Meet the Kit

■ The modern-day cat evolved from Miacids, small tree-climbing creatures, that roamed the earth about 61 million years ago.

■ Historians estimate that the first domestication of the cat occurred in Egypt as early as 3,500 to 4,000 years ago.

■ All cats are members of the Felidea order of species. *Felidea* is comprised of three classifications of cats: *Panthera*, *Felis* and *Aninonyx*. *Felis* is the genus that includes non-roaring cats, and today's domestic cats.

■ In the early part of the century, cats earned their keep in North America by policing haylofts and barnyards and by running pest control in city warehouses.

■ Cats moved into the parlor after kitty litter was invented in the 1940s.

■ Cats come in a variety of patterns and colors, which include calico, tabby, pointed, snow white, tipping, agouti and tuxedo.

■ Cats sleep about 16 hours a day!

■ The cat's games are all variations of hunting, fighting and mating behaviors.

■ Contrary to popular belief, cats are highly trainable and learn obedience quickly and easily.

Consulting Editor

BETSY SIKORA SIINO

Featuring Photographs by

ERIC ILASENKO

Copyright © 1999, 1998 by Wiley Publishing, Inc., New York, NY
Copyright © 1999 all photography by Winter Churchill Photography unless
otherwise noted

Howell Book House
Published by Wiley Publishing, Inc., New York, NY

The Essential Kitten is a revised edition of *Kitten Care and Training: An
Owner's Guide to a Happy Healthy Pet*, first published in 1996.

ISBN 1-58245-075-7

LOC 99-62790

Manufactured in the United States of America
10 9 8 7 6 5 4

Series Director: Michele Matrisciani
Production Team: Heather Pope, Kristi Hart and Terri Sheehan
Book Design: Paul Costello
Photography: Eric Ilasenko
Cover Photo by: Mary Bloom

ARE YOU READY?!

☐ Have you prepared your home and your family for your new pet?

☐ Have you gotten the proper supplies you'll need to care for your kitten?

☐ Have you found a veterinarian that you (and your kitten) are comfortable with?

☐ Have you thought about how you want your kitten to behave?

☐ Have you arranged your schedule to accommodate your kitten's needs for exercise and attention?

No matter what stage you're at with your kitten—still thinking about getting one, or he's already part of the family—this Essential guide will provide you with the practical information you need to understand and care for your feline companion. Of course you're ready—you have this book!

THE
ESSENTIAL

Kitten

The Kitten's Senses

SIGHT

As hunters, cats rely on vision to find prey. In fact, cats have the largest eyes of any carnivore, proportional to head size.

SOUND

Cats respond better to high-pitched voices perhaps because they can't hear low pitches as well as people can. But cats out-hear people in higher ranges.

TASTE

The cat's tongue is flexible and curls at the tip, acting like a ladle and scooping up water with every lick. Because they establish their eating habits at an early age, cats tend to prefer to stick to a familiar diet.

TOUCH

Touch is a pleasurable sensation to cats, and is important both physically and emotionally. Pleasurable touch, such as petting, promotes relaxation and reduces stress—for both of you.

SMELL

Despite a small head, cats have a greater number of scent-analyzing cells than humans do. Your kitten's nose also serves a protective function: It filters, warms and humidifies air and traps bacteria as a defense against infection.

CHAPTER ONE

Getting to Know Your Kitten

Although every cat shares the same qualities and physical characteristics that define him as a cat, each feline is also unique. Kittens come in a variety of distinctive coat colors, patterns and hair lengths, and even their body shapes vary. Certain features are most apparent in pure-bred cats, but every cat, even the new kitten frisking about your feet, leans toward a certain feline "type."

THE OUTER PACKAGE

Non-pedigreed kitties are categorized by the length of their fur as either Domestic Shorthair (DSH) or Domestic Longhair (DLH) cats. Coat length runs the gamut from extremely short, satinlike fur, to luxurious flowing tresses. Some cats even have unusual wavy or crinkly "wire hair" coats.

The coat is composed of four types of hairs. The soft undercoat that keeps Kitty warm is called down. Middle-length hairs, called awn hairs, insulate and protect the skin, while the longest, thickest hairs are guard hairs making up the protective outer

There are many varieties of kittens. Pictured here from left to right: a Domestic Shorthair brown tabby kitten (a), a Persian red tabby (b), a seal point Siamese (c), a tortoiseshell Persian kitten (d) and a shorthair white and black kitty (e).

coat. The whiskers are wirelike vibrissae found mostly on the face but also on the back of the legs.

COAT COLOR

Coat color adds even more variety. Solid-color kittens are striking and range from black, dark gray (called blue), brown or light gray (called lilac) to red, cream or snow white. Bicolor patterns are two distinct solid colors, like the striking black and white "tuxedo cats."

Tortoiseshell and calico coloring appear only rarely in male cats. A tortoiseshell kitten is black with red streaks or patches, and white cats with patches of red and black are called calico.

Some solid-color kittens sport shaded fur, which means the tip of each hair is darker or lighter than the rest of the hair. Tipping adds a sparkling or smoky shimmer to the coat. Agouti coloring looks like rabbit fur, where each individual hair is banded with various colors. Abyssinian cats have agouti coloring that ranges from fawn to deep red, brown or even blue.

The Siamese cat is best known for his pointed pattern, in which his tail, legs and muzzle are darker than his light-color body. Longhair cats, like the Himalayan, also may have dark points.

Tabby is not a breed of cat. The term describes the dark-on-light markings that occur in nearly every color. The mackerel tabby sports a

tiger-stripe pattern, while the classic tabby has a marbled look. In the spotted tabby, the kitten's body is covered with spots, while tail and lower limbs are striped. Some cats even have interesting combinations of tabby patterns.

FUR FUNCTION

Besides being beautiful, healthy fur is a protective barrier between your kitten's body and the environment. Well-groomed fur falls in smooth, loose-lying layers that insulate. During severe cold, saliva from grooming smoothes the hair coat so that it becomes a more efficient insulator, helping to maintain body heat.

Perspiring is one way of lowering body temperature when overheated, and, like other mammals, cats have sweat glands. But only the specialized eccrine glands produce watery sweat like ours, and they're located on Kitty's paw pads. These sweat glands aren't particularly effective for heat loss. Instead, self-grooming helps the cat cool off.

By keeping his coat free of mats, the cat can elevate and "fluff" his fur, which opens the coat and allows air to pass between the hairs. This can either cool the skin or allow in extra heat. When very hot, cats also pant to cool themselves, but as much as a third of the evaporative-cooling process occurs when the cat licks his skin and hair. Evaporation of saliva spread on the fur by grooming is an extremely effective means of keeping cool.

Self-grooming also helps the cat maintain healthy skin. Tugging at the hair coat stimulates sebaceous glands in the skin at the base of the individual hairs, which produce sebum. Sebum lubricates and waterproofs fur, and is spread by the cat's tongue when he grooms himself. Sebum also contains cholesterol, which is converted by sunlight into vitamin D. It is through washing that Kitty absorbs much of his nutritional requirement of vitamin D, which contributes to healthy bones and teeth, and aids calcium and phosphorus absorption and utilization.

BODY TYPE

Most DSH and DLH kittens have the domestic body type, an average-appearing yet muscular body. Persian cats typify the cobby body type, with a flattened face, round head and eyes, and short thick legs. The third general body type is the foreign model, which is a more lightly built, very slim cat with larger ears, slanted eyes and a longer, narrower muzzle, like the Siamese. Does your kitten tend toward the foreign or cobby body type? He may have Siamese or Persian in his background, respectively.

Even tails vary from cat to cat. Most DSH and DLH cats have long, supple tails. A kitten may be born with a short thick tail, a twisted puffy bunny tail or no tail at all. Tail-less breeds of cats include the Manx, the American Bobtail and the Japanese Bobtail. If your kitten is a tail-less wonder, perhaps it's because of a tail-less ancestor.

5

BOY OR GIRL?

A furry body may hide things you want to know. It's sometimes hard to tell whether you've adopted a boy or girl kitten. Lift your kitten's tail to determine gender. The position of a female's anus and vulva resembles an upside down exclamation point, while a male's furry behind looks more like a colon. As your boy matures, his testicles will become more apparent.

A FELINE SLINKY

Despite distinctive coats, cats are very similar under the fur. Muscles holding the skeleton together give cats an incredible range of movement. That's because cats have 5 more vertebrae than people do, with the extras behind the shoulders. Seven cervical, 13 thoracic, 7 lumbar and three sacral vertebrae held together by muscles instead of ligaments make your kitten very muscular.

For this kitten, a few licks to the paw are simply instinctive.

Shoulder blades located on his sides enable your kitten to move his front legs in nearly every direction. His shoulder blades are attached to muscle rather than to a collarbone. This increases the cat's extreme elasticity.

FEET AND CLAWS

If it seems your kitten "tippy-toes," you're right. Cats are digitigrade: They walk on their toes. This, combined with the unique shoulder blade location, gives Kitty a long, fluid stride.

Catch Kitty now while you can, because when he grows up, he'll run nearly 30 miles an hour. Tails are used for balance during high-speed turns and when exploring precarious heights. In fact, many domestic cats are exceptional jumpers and climbers who can jump five times their own height.

Curved claws allow Kitty to climb as quickly as he runs on the ground. It's not so easy coming down, though, and cats often mew for help or shimmy backward down the tree.

Cat claws, made of keratin, grow from the last bone of each toe. Because they never stop growing, claws often need clipping just like human fingernails. Claws retract beneath the skin when Kitty is relaxed, and they extend when Kitty flexes his muscles, contracting the tendons and

Kittens are muscular and flexible

The kitties in this basket are settling down for their first catnap of the day.

7

straightening the toes. Some cats even have extra toes, called poly-dactylism. If your kitten is a "mitten cat" with extra toes, he inherited them from his parents.

Although full of energy, your kitten needs frequent naps. Even adult cats typically sleep up to 16 hours a day. However, about 70 percent of that rest is spent in light catnaps, during which Kitty remains aware of scents, sounds and the world around him.

SENSE OF TOUCH

One of the first sensations your kitten experienced was his mother's tongue washing and massaging his furry little body. Touch is a pleasurable sensation to cats, and it is important both physically and emotionally. Petting your kitten not only lowers your own blood pressure, it does the same for the cat. Pleasurable touch promotes relaxation and reduces stress.

Tiny pressure-sensitive lumps are scattered over the cat's body, making the entire skin very touch-sensitive. Your kitten enjoys being stroked, but he can feel even indirect contact. A single hair being disturbed will trigger a response in the pressure point nearest that hair—and alert your kitten.

How Whiskers Work

Because stiff whiskers (vibrissae) are set much deeper in the skin than other hair, they are extremely sensitive and act like a kind of kitty antennae. Whiskers help protect the eyes, too, by triggering a blink reflex when something brushes them. Cat whiskers are also sensitive to air pressure and currents in relation to close objects, which helps Kitty judge distance.

When your kitten curiously sticks his head into a small opening, whiskers tell him whether he'll fit through the space. And in darkness, whiskers on his face and legs help him avoid danger.

Just as young children poke fingers and grab objects, cats use their paws

The hairless bottoms of your kitten's feet, the paw pads and the tip of his nose are the most sensitive to touch.

to tap and prod things to see whether they're safe.

Cats love warmth and can bear temperatures as high as 125°F before registering discomfort. Your kitten may, in fact, seem insensitive to heat; some kitties suffer a singed tail without reacting. But the cat can tell slight differences of a degree or two simply by touching the object with his sensitive nose.

SENSE OF TASTE

Taste isn't nearly as important to cats as smell, although the two senses are closely linked and register in the same area of the brain. Taste buds on the edges of the tongue and inside the mouth and lips detect sour, salt, sweet and bitter just as ours do.

Down the center of the tongue are rows of hooked, backward-pointing projections called papillae. But newborns have only a rim of papillae around the edge of the tongue for grasping their mother's nipple when they nurse.

The adult kitty tongue rasps food and is also used as a grooming tool and to collect liquids when Kitty drinks. The curled tongue becomes a kitty spoon for drinking; lapping cats typically swallow after every four or five laps.

Kittens have 26 baby teeth that are lost from 12 weeks to 6 months of age and are replaced by 30 adult teeth. But cats don't use teeth to chew. They turn their head to one side, and use teeth to grasp and shear food into swallowable portions.

SENSE OF SMELL

Aroma identifies life for our cats; without scent, the cat would be lost. Newborns use scent to find their mother, stake out a preferred nipple and return time after time to the same scent-marked place. From birth on, Kitty is led around by the nose.

The outside ridged pattern of your kitten's nose leather is unique, like a fingerprint. His nose is part of the upper respiratory tract and includes the nostrils (nares) and the interior nasal cavity that runs the length of the muzzle. Open spaces in the bone, called sinuses, connect to the nasal cavity.

The nasal cavity is enclosed by bone and cartilage, and it is divided by a midline partition into two passages, one for each nostril, that open into the throat behind the soft

AGE AND LIFE SPAN

How does a cat's age compare with a human's? When your cat is 1 year old, he's 15 in human years; at 2, he's 25; and it slows down from there, averaging about an additional 3 years each during a cat's teens and 20s. Therefore, when your cat is 14, he's 72 human years old, and at the ripe age of 19, he's 87.

palate. The partition, called the nasal septum, is a vertical plate made of bone and cartilage.

How Smell Works

A series of rolled, bony plates called turbinates are found inside the nasal cavity. The sense of smell originates with olfactory cells and nerves located in the olfactory mucosa, 3 to 6 square inches of thick, spongy membrane that covers the turbinates.

Despite a small head, cats have a much greater number of scent-analyzing cells than humans. People have 5 to 20 million such cells, while your kitten has 67 million.

Odors enter the nose as fine airborne particles. Millions of tiny hairlike receptors extend from the olfactory cells into the thin layer of mucus that keeps the area

9

moist. Odor particles are dissolved in the moisture, then make contact with the receptors. The dissolved odor particles stimulate olfactory nerves to signal the olfactory bulbs, which are directly linked to the brain. Once in the brain, exactly how smell is interpreted remains a mystery.

Your kitten's nose is not only a scenting organ, but also serves a protective function. The scroll-like structures inside the nose increase the surface area that filters, warms and humidifies air. Glands throughout the nasal cavity form secretions that maintain moisture levels inside the nose. This protective coating traps bacteria and foreign bodies as a defense against infection.

Without his keen sense of smell, the cat would be lost.

Extra Scent Organs

Cats also have extra scent organs, called Jacobson's organs, or vomeronasal organs. They specialize in scents that stimulate behavioral responses, especially sexual responses.

The vomeronasal organs are found in the mouth, between the hard palate and the nasal septum. Each organ is linked to incisive ducts that connect the oral cavity to the nasal cavity. The ducts open behind Kitty's upper incisor teeth and permit air in the mouth to pass up into the nasal cavity.

To use these organs, Kitty traps scent particles on his tongue and then transfers them to the ducts behind his upper teeth. This behavior, common in horses too, is known by the German term *flehmen*, roughly translated as "lip-curl." The cat seems to grimace with mouth open and upper lip curled back, but what looks like repulsion actually indicates enthusiastic interest.

Flehmen is performed mainly by intact adult males, and it most often happens when they find the urine of a sexually receptive female kitty. Female cats also flehmen under certain conditions, and the behavior has been seen in kittens as young as two months.

SENSE OF SIGHT

Sight is probably the most important sense for cats. As hunters, cats rely on vision to find prey. In fact, cats have the largest eyes of any carnivore. If human eye-to-face ratio were the same as Kitty's, your eyes would be 8 inches across!

Feline eye size and location provide almost 280 degrees of three-dimensional sight. A cat's peripheral vision is sharper than his straight-ahead vision. Kitties are quite near-sighted, and they see motion more easily than stationary objects.

Cats see extremely well in the dark because they only need one-sixth the illumination level and use twice as much available light as people. Light reflects off the mirrorlike tapetum lucidum, a layer of cells at the back of the cat's eye, and is reflected back through the retina to augment vision. It's this reflected light that causes the eerie night shine we see in glowing feline eyes.

The colored area of your kitten's eye is the iris, which is a figure-eight muscle that regulates how much light passes through. The iris is able to quickly open (dilate) the pupil into a circle when the light is low, and to shut it tight into a fine vertical slit in

THE EYES HAVE IT

A cat's eyes are truly unique. They are large and seated deep within the skull. This limits the amount the eyeball can move, but it allows for excellent peripheral vision, especially of moving objects. That is why the cat will dart its head to the side once he has detected movement from the side.

The vertical pupil responds quickly to changes in light, enlarging in the dark and closing to a slit in bright light. Cats are somewhat nearsighted; they can't see close-up objects too well. The pupils also close to a slit to help cats focus on nearby objects. Cats can see a limited range of colors.

All cat owners know that their kitty's eyes are hypnotic. They're the stuff of myth and legend, and they even have a gemstone (Cat's-Eye) named after them. This stone has been used to protect people from witchcraft, make people invisible and prevent women from getting pregnant when their husbands were away.

Cats have the largest eyes of any carnivore, proportionate to head size.

Cats' ears are designed to pick up high-pitched noises—like the squeak of a mouse.

11

bright light. Light passes through the pupil and is focussed by the lens onto the retina at the back of the eye. Light-sensitive receptors on the

180 degrees and is used to funnel sound waves into the auditory canal. There, the fragile membrane of the eardrum resonates when struck by sound waves. The vibration is amplified by a complex system of tiny bones and fluid-filled tubes of the inner ear. Then, signals are transmitted to the brain, where they are interpreted as sound.

BALANCING ACT

The vestibular apparatus of the inner ear also gives your kitten his uncanny sense of balance. Coupled with vision and the elastic strength of his spine, Kitty's innate equilibrium allows him to become an acrobat during falls. He twists and turns in midair to land nearly always on his feet.

For the righting mechanism to work properly, however, cats must be awake, and they must have enough distance in which to turn. Falls from very short heights, like from a child's arms, may not give Kitty enough time to turn. And falls from heights that are too great can result in broken legs and a split jaw when Kitty hits the ground, even if he makes a perfect four-foot landing.

Cats have the largest eyes of any carnivore.

surface of the retina transfer signals through the optic nerve to the brain, where the information is translated into vision.

SENSE OF HEARING

Cats respond better to high-pitched voices perhaps because they can't hear low pitches as well as people can. But cats, especially youngsters like your kitten, out-hear people in the higher ranges. This allows Kitty to detect high-pitched mouse squeaks of up to 60,000 cycles per second. People with the sharpest ears can hear only about 20,000 cycles per second.

In the ear, the furred portion you see, called the pina, can rotate

CHAPTER TWO

Homecoming

When it comes to fun, nothing beats a kitten. But the feline "wonder years" can also be the most frustrating and dangerous time in your kitten's life. Don't let Kitty's innocent face fool you. Behind those twinkling bright eyes is a mind brimful of curiosity, and the boundless energy to try to satisfy it. Kittens have a way of turning the most innocuous situation into a disaster. Whether you survive with your sanity intact—and whether your kitten survives at all—can depend on your kitten-proofing your home.

KITTEN-PROOFING THE HOUSE

An indoors-only living arrangement is safest for all cats, and the first step toward making this a success is to kitten-proof the house so that Kitty doesn't hurt herself. It also prevents her from laying waste to your house so that you don't yearn to retaliate.

First, try to think like a cat. Invest in kneepads, get down on all fours and tour your house at kitten level. But jumping and climbing kittens rarely stop at floor level, so

POISONOUS PLANTS

The following house- and outdoor plants contain substances that are poisonous to cats. If chewed or ingested, these plants can cause symptoms ranging from vomiting and diarrhea to rapid heartbeat, kidney problems or even death.

- Azalea
- Bird of Paradise
- Black Locust
- Chrysanthemum
- Daffodil
- Elephant Ears
- Ivy
- Jack-in-the-Pulpit
- Larkspur
- Marijuana
- Nutmeg
- Poinsettia
- Rhubarb
- Skunk Cabbage

reach is fair game, so place anything breakable out of feline range. The more intelligent the kitten, the more ways she'll find to get into trouble.

Toxic Houseplants

Protect your kitten from houseplants . . . and vice versa. To a kitten, a large floor plant is an exotic jungle gym to scale, while a pot of soil is an invitation to furry excavators.

Chewing houseplants like dieffenbachia, philodendron, pothos and English ivy can cause toxic reactions. Kitty may even lick off the poison when she grooms her claws after shredding the plant. Keep plants out of your kitten's reach by hanging them or placing them on inaccessible shelves. Choose non-toxic plants like the jade plant, the prayer plant, the begonia, donkey tail, coleus or piggyback.

Securing Cords

Kittens don't tend to chew as much as puppies, but they do play-attack and bite nearly everything. Electric cords can be particularly tempting, and bitten cords can result in severe burns or even death. Get rid of or hide as many electrical cords as

you also need to kitten-proof the heights.

Despite evidence to the contrary, kittens do not have hands. Instead, they use patting paws to explore their world, and they stick their tiny noses into everything. Anything left within possible, and check remaining wires regularly for signs of chewing. Tape cords to the floor to keep them from moving (and reduce Kitty's temptation to bat and bite them).

Trash and Other Items

Keep garbage away from your kitten. Although cats are generally more fastidious than their canine counterparts, the smell of scraps may tempt Kitty to scrounge. Your kitten might be poisoned by eating potato eyes or chocolate, or she might end up with an upset stomach that results in a predictable mess. Securely fasten lids on trash containers, or store them under the sink or in the garage where the kitten can't reach them. Don't leave sharp knives, food-processor blades or other utensils out on counters where Kitty might try to lick them clean—and cut her tongue.

Like children, kittens have a tendency to swallow small nonfood items like coins, pins, erasers and paper clips. Anything left out is fair game for the cat. Carefully cap all medications, and put them away. Pills are fun to bat around the floor, but if swallowed they can be poisonous. Aspirin and Tylenol™ are deadly to cats!

Decoration Disasters

Christmas is an enchanting yet dangerous time of year for kittens. The tree seems meant for climbing, and the blinking lights and swinging ornaments tempt even the most stoic kitty to indulge. But broken ornaments, extra electric cords, metal hooks or tinsel, sprayed lead-base "snow" and tree needles all pose dangers. Avoid placing decorations on the bottom branches; be sure the tree is securely anchored; avoid tinsel; and use ribbon to hang unbreakable ornaments.

Toys and Strings

Carefully inspect cat toys, and remove small eyes or tails that could come

This DSH bats at her favorite feather toy, which is safe and fun for kitties.

15

require surgical removal. Tie up curtain cords out of kitten reach, or purchase breakaway cords. The standard double cords on window blinds can hang and strangle a kitten.

Hiding Places

Kittens and adult cats delight in cubbyholes in which to sleep. Always check cupboards and dresser drawers before shutting them to be sure your kitten isn't hiding inside. Keep appliances closed. Kitty may think she's found the perfect warm hidy-hole to sleep—until the appliance is turned on. It may sound funny at first, but kittens die every day by being accidentally shut inside a dishwasher, washing machine, clothes dryer or stove.

Watch where you step! Sometimes your kitten's tiny size is her own worst hazard, allowing her to easily get under foot.

Your kitten will never cease to find new hiding places.

Fire

Fire will cause either fear or fascination in your kitten, and patting paws will get burned if she tries to catch the flame. Cats like warm places to sleep but may get singed when allowed unsupervised access to hot stove burners, irons or lit fireplaces.

loose and be swallowed. Put away sewing baskets and tackle boxes. Kittens love to play with thread, string and yarn, but unsupervised games can lead to accidental strangulation, swallowed needles, cuts from fishing line or embedded fish hooks. Cats can swallow several yards of ribbon or string, which will

Protect your sanity—and your new kitten's life—by running

interference for the little one and by clearing lethal booby traps out of your house. Then sit back, relax and treasure the antics of the furry wonder who now shares your life. Kittenhood doesn't last forever, but kittenproofing your home will ensure that the memories you make today will be happy ones. And happy kitty memories are oh-so-sweet, sweet enough to last a lifetime.

FOOD AND WATER DISHES

Every kitten should have her own set of dishes. A variety of styles is available at most pet supply outlets, or even grocery stores. Your kitten probably won't care whether her bowls are plain or elaborate,

KITTY'S BASIC NEEDS

These are the things all kittens need, and you're better off getting them before your kitten comes home so that you're prepared.

food dish   identification tag

water dish   grooming tools

cat carrier   litter tray

collar   bed

first-aid kit

but a number of cute styles are available to tickle any pet-lover's fancy.

A minimum of two bowls is needed. One holds water, while the second is for food. Some owners settle for one dish for water and use

17

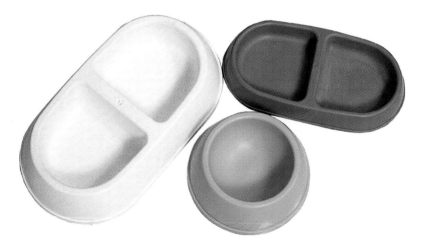

Some types of food and water bowls available for your kitten.

COLLARING KITTY

All cats, even those kept exclusively indoors, should wear a collar with identification. It takes just a moment for your new kitten to slip out the door, and tags can help ensure her safe return if she becomes lost.

However, the cat's delicate neck can be easily injured by ill-fitting or poorly designed collars. Collars that catch on objects can hang and strangle the cat. Choose a collar designed with elastic inserts that stretch to release tangled cats. Collars should fit snugly, with room for two fingers to fit easily underneath. Sometimes the size of a cat's neck isn't much different from the size of her head; so even a properly fitting collar may tend to slide off.

Never, ever attach the leash to a cat's collar. A hysterical cat can leap and quite literally break her neck. A cagey cat may simply turn and back away, pull the collar off, and disappear. A harness and leash are the proper cat-walking equipment.

The preferred harness for cats is either a lightweight figure-H or figure-eight halter. One strap goes around the cat's neck, while the other wraps about her body behind the forelegs. The leash should be lightweight cloth, nylon or leather, no longer than 6 feet. The leash is attached to a metal ring in the harness above the cat's shoulders.

disposable paper plates for each kitty meal.

The perfect cat dish is heavy enough that Kitty won't have to "follow" it all over the room as she eats, and it is balanced so that it won't tip over. Shallow, wide bowls that have plenty of whisker room get feline raves. Cats don't like scrunching their whiskers or getting themselves dirty by diving headfirst into a deep bowl. Be sure to buy bowls that will still please your kitten when she's adult size.

Food dishes must be easy to wash to remove odors that might offend delicate cat noses. Plastic dishes are hard to get clean, and some cats may have allergic reactions to them. Stainless steel dishes won't chip, crack or break; they're easy to clean and dishwasher-safe; but they may be too lightweight. Ceramic or glass dishes are much better—and answer the needs of most cats.

THE LITTER BOX

What goes in one end of the kitten as food and water must be dealt with at the other end. Standard kitten equipment includes a litter box, a slotted scoop and litter.

Kitty's bathroom facilities should be large enough for her to turn around easily, but not so large that she can't see over the sides. Pans should be deep enough to hold at least 2 inches of litter for digging, but not be so shallow that she tosses litter onto the floor. Adult cats should have no trouble stepping into the box. Very young kittens may need to be helped into the box until they "grow" into the facilities.

Most commercial litter pans are about 5 × 12 × 18 inches and are made of easily cleaned plastic. These are generally fine for kittens. If your kitten grows into a monster cat or if you have two cats who agree to share, larger pans are available. As with food bowls, all kinds of colors and styles of litter pans are available in pet stores and mail-order catalogs. Covered models reduce the litter that enthusiastic diggers fling out of the box, and they also offer Kitty some privacy.

Types of Litter

The most popular litter today is clay-based granules that feel good to digging cat feet, absorb moisture and odor and have a minimum of dust or tracking. Many brands are available, and new ones appear every day.

"Scoopable" litters are extremely convenient because liquid waste congeals into firm balls that can be lifted out of the pan to prolong the life of the rest of the litter. Some litters can also be flushed—even more convenient.

19

The different varieties of litter are (l-r): clay-based litter, scoopable or clumping litter and natural pelleted litter.

This litter box is just the right size for this little girl.

Other litters, like pelleted litter, are made of recycled paper, wheat, cedar shavings and other biodegradable products. What works for one cat may not appeal to another. When choosing a litter, remember that cats prefer sandy, soil-like textures with no perfumes or dust.

Slotted litter scoops lift waste from the soiled box but allow clean litter to sift back into the box. Commercial scoops are available, but any slotted spoon or spatula will work. If your litter isn't flushable or your septic system can't handle litter, keep a covered wastebasket or diaper pail handy to deposit Kitty's offerings. A whisk broom or hand vacuum is helpful to clean up tracked litter.

Spray deodorants may make you feel better, but they will scare your kitten and offend her scent sense, too. The best way to handle litter box odor is to keep the box clean.

FOR YOUR KITTEN'S COMFORT

Felines spend much of their lives sleeping, and they're most comfortable on a warm, cozy surface. There is a variety of cat beds on the market, available in numerous sizes, shapes and colors. Experiment with those if you like, or make your own soft spot for your kitten. This can be as simple as a special blanket in Kitty's favorite spots, wherever those may be—a special chair, a window-sill, the top of the clothes dryer or your bed. Washable blankets are best. Your kitten will let you know which fabrics she prefers.

Because cats relish the view from the windowsill (of a closed window), you may want to construct a special perch at a particularly favored win-dow. The perch could be small or large, depending on how you want to design it—anything from a carpet-lined plank to curl up on to a climbing station with a view. Pet supply stores and catalogs will give you ideas.

FOR YOUR KITTEN'S FUN

You'll want to have a supply of toys for your kitten to keep her occupied—and you'll want to share this activity with her. With a kitten's fascination for moving objects, it's not hard to come up with simple, fun toys. An all-time favorite is the kitty fishing rod. To a 2- or 3-foot pole, attach a foot-long length of twine or strong string to which

BEDTIME

Your kitten should have a safe place to which she can retire and not be disturbed. Count-less designer cat beds are available, from fleece-lined teepees and tunnels to nestlike cat lounges or even kitty hammocks.

However, a soft, cuddly blanket inside her cat carrier may just as easily tickle your kitten's fancy. Often, the kitten chooses where she wants to sleep. You may need to gently dissuade her if you don't want to share your pillow.

Fireplaces are dangerous play areas for kittens. This silver Persian scampers through the fire-place accessories.

you've tied a large feather, a stuffed sock or a small ball. From the com-fort of your chair, you can play "fish" with your kitten, who will spend hours chasing and catching the object at the end of the pole.

GROOMING SUPPLES

There are basic grooming tools all cat owners should have. Types of brushes vary depending on whether your cat has short hair (SH) or long hair (LH). Basic tools include:

soft-bristle brush (SH)

natural or wire slicker brush (LH)

rubber curry brush (SH)

stainless steel wide-tooth comb (LH)

fine-tooth flea comb

cat nail clippers

flea shampoo

baby oil

cotton balls

commercial ear-cleaning solution

gauze pads

saline solution

A look through any pet supply store or catalog will supply you with a slew of ideas for toys you can buy or make. Cats love to explore, and so cardboard boxes with cutaway entrances make great toys. There are fabric-lined tubes you can buy for your kitty to run through, as well as a host of squeaky, fleecy and bouncy toys.

Another favorite amusement is catnip. The plant itself is a member of the mint family, and the chemical it contains gets kitties going. That chemical is nepetalactone; it triggers something in the scent glands that has a euphoric effect on cats. They respond by licking, chewing or rubbing the plant or a catnip-filled toy. Like mint, catnip is fairly easy to grow, and you can plant your own crop from which to pick and dry leaves. Or, you can buy dried catnip and already-made toys in pet supply stores.

SCRATCHING POSTS

Cats scratch. Period. There is no way to stop it, and even declawed cats go through the motions. Therefore, a proper scratching object is a necessity.

Because many owners don't understand why the cat scratches, they choose a scratching object that Kitty refuses to use. Cat claws, like human fingernails, grow constantly. Dragging claws through rough fabric like upholstery or carpet helps remove the outer sheath and makes room for new growth. It's also great exercise that simply feels good, and cats often scratch to express happiness or to mark territory.

Your kitten basically is looking for a nail file that's tall enough or long enough to give her muscles a good, stretching workout. The scratching object must be sturdy and stable enough that a full kitty assault won't knock it over.

Many carpet-covered scratching posts are available that match any decor, but don't let simple looks sway you. If the scratching object doesn't meet Kitty's criteria, she'll find something that does, like the living room sofa, the plaster wall or a chair leg.

What to Look For

The best commercial scratching posts have a rough cover that files Kitty's nails; sisal, tree bark or very

dense carpet work well. Choose a post that your kitten won't outgrow. Make sure it doesn't slide around or tip over when she's using it, or Kitty may never go near the post again. Scratching posts are available in pet supply stores or through mail order.

This kitten reclines in a window hammock, which provides a safe view of the outside.

Just a few of the most popular kitty toys available to entertain your pet.

A blue and white Persian and a flame point Himalayan exercise their scratching skills on a carpet-covered cat tree.

Some cats relish homemade scratching objects. A piece of cordwood from the fireplace is the simplest way to go. For the ambitious, use carpet remnants and mount them wrong side out on a plywood sheet or wooden post. Any of these can be secured against the wall, on a wooden base or simply left flat on the floor for horizontal scratchers.

THE TRAVELING CAT

Even exclusively indoor cats must occasionally make a trip to the groomer or veterinarian. A variety of versatile, safe cat carriers are available, and a carrier should always be used even when Kitty is traveling short distances.

Some cats get so upset while traveling that they may have accidents, and confining them to a carrier makes cleanups much easier. More importantly, your distraught kitten could slip through your arms on the way to the car and become lost. Kittens and cats allowed to roam in a moving car can cause injury to themselves or others by blocking the driver's view or getting under his feet.

The carrier you choose should be large enough for the adult cat to turn around in, yet not so large that Kitty rattles about like salt in a shaker. Cats prefer quarters that make them feel secure. The hard plastic airline-approved carriers are very safe and readily available. Space-capsule-type carriers or soft-sided duffle-type bags with zippers are also popular. Inexpensive cardboard carriers are usually available at pet stores or veterinarians. Confining Kitty to a cat carrier while traveling is safest for all concerned. If possible, secure the carrier with a seat belt.

CHAPTER THREE

To Good Health

Your kitten's health depends on the working partnership between you and your veterinarian. To start off on the right paw, your kitten should be evaluated by a veterinarian as soon as you get him.

You must feel comfortable with your veterinarian, who should always be willing to answer your questions.

Only then will it be a true partnership that best benefits your kitten.

Advances in feline health and medicine are constantly being made. This chapter is only a guide and is meant to help you diagnose and understand your kitten's ailments; always consult your veterinarian for the most current information.

PREVENTIVE HEALTH CARE

Prevention is truly the best cure and should be used to ensure a happy, healthy life for your new kitten. The idea is simple: Prevent illnesses from developing or spreading by following basic health-care principles. These include vaccinating your kitten against infectious diseases; keeping routine appointments with your veterinarian so he or she can monitor the overall health of your kitten; and keeping close tabs on your kitten yourself, checking skin, teeth, fur, eyes, ears and mood. These simple preventive procedures will save you dollars, time and heartache.

Vaccinations

To be fully protected, your kitten needs a series of vaccinations 2 to 3 weeks apart, starting when he's 6 to 8 weeks old and continuing until he's 14 to 16 weeks of age. Once the series has been completed, yearly vaccinations protect adult cats thereafter. Currently, four vaccinations are available to protect your kitten from preventable illnesses.

A combination shot protects the kitten against feline distemper and

WHEN TO CALL YOUR VETERINARIAN

In any emergency situation, you should call your veterinarian immediately. You can make the difference in your kitten's life by staying as calm as possible when you call and by giving the doctor or assistant as much information as possible before you leave for the clinic. That way, your veterinarian will be able to take immediate, specific action to remedy your kitten's situation.

Emergencies include acute abdominal pain, suspected poisoning, burns, frostbite, dehydration, shock, abnormal vomiting or bleeding and deep wounds. You should also consult your veterinarian if your kitten has a thick discharge from eyes or nose, is coughing or sneezing, refuses food or has a change in bathroom habits. Never give your kitten human medication unless instructed to do so by your veterinarian.

You are the best judge of your kitten's health because you live with and observe him every day. If you notice changes—such as lethargy, which may indicate a fever caused by infection—don't hesitate to call your veterinarian. Normal cat temperature is 101° to 102.5°F; anything higher indicates illness.

upper respiratory virus diseases. A three-in-one vaccination combines protection against feline distemper, feline calicivirus and feline

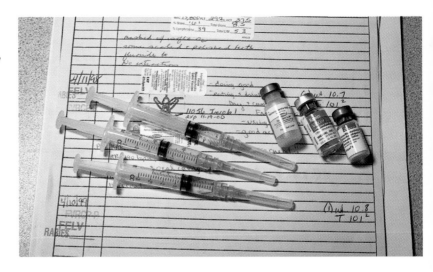

This is the vaccine history of one healthy kitty and syringes filled with the most common cat vaccines.

herpesvirus. And a four-in-one includes feline chlamydiosis.

The FeLV vaccination protects cats against feline leukemia virus

KITTY NO-NOS

We are so used to taking aspirin, ibuprofen and acetaminophen when we feel bad that it's tempting to give the same to our pets when they're feeling bad. But no matter how tempted you might be, *never* give your cat these medications. All are toxic to cats, even in one-pill doses. If you suspect your kitten has eaten these or other human medications, or any other kind of poison, call your veterinarian and the National Animal Poison Control Center (800-548-2423).

infection. Initially, a small sample of your kitten's blood is tested to be sure he's healthy, since FeLV won't protect him if he's already infected with the disease. When the result is negative, the kitten receives two vaccinations about three weeks apart and then is revaccinated yearly thereafter.

The FIP vaccination against feline infectious peritonitis initially requires two doses three to four weeks apart, and then yearly thereafter. Unlike the others, the FIP vaccine is not an injection, but rather is administered as nose drops.

A rabies vaccination is recommended for all cats and is required by law in many states. Kittens typically are first given a rabies shot at age 16 weeks, then are revaccinated either annually or every three years, depending on the local vaccine and the laws.

COMMON DISEASES

Upper Respiratory Infection

Cats are susceptible to upper respiratory infections because they inhale viruses and bacteria as they sniff interesting odors.

The most common sign is sneezing, but coughing, runny eyes and nose and even painful eye and mouth ulcers can develop. Severe disease can lead to pneumonia. There is no cure; treatment is limited to symptomatic and supportive care. Recovered cats become carriers for life and can transmit the disease to other healthy cats during "flare-ups" brought on by stress.

Disease is primarily spread by direct cat-to-cat contact, aerosol (sneezing) and contact with contaminated items, like cages, food bowls and litter boxes. The virus can also be carried on human skin, which means you can spread the infection by simply petting your cats.

Feline Distemper

This type of feline parvovirus is not related to canine distemper. Signs include depression, fever, loss of appetite, diarrhea, vomiting and dehydration. Ninety to 100 percent of unvaccinated cats who are exposed to the virus will die.

Choosing a veterinarian who truly seems to care for your kitten.

Recovered cats may become carriers able to infect other unprotected cats. The virus is extremely contagious and is transmitted orally through contact with infected surfaces like food bowls or litter boxes. The virus can live in the environment for months or even years, and it is resistant to most common disinfectants.

Feline Leukemia Virus (FeLV)

The leading infectious cause of death in cats in the United States, feline leukemia virus compromises the cat's immune system, making FeLV-infected cats more susceptible to other diseases. Most cats die within three years of infection from related diseases like leukemia (cancer of the blood cells), cancer of the lymph system or anemia.

Any major medical problem can indicate FeLV infection. But infected cats may show no symptoms for years, yet can be shedding the virus and infecting other cats. The disease is spread by cat-to-cat contact, through shared dishes and litter boxes or even from an

This owner looks on while the veterinarian gives her new kitten a full physical.

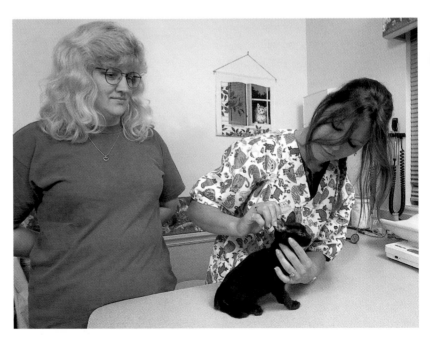

infected mother cat to her unborn kittens.

The virus is extremely fragile and does not survive long in the environment. It can be destroyed by common household products like detergents, alcohol and bleach. Preventing contact with strange cats eliminates exposure.

Feline Infectious Peritonitis (FIP)

Feline infectious peritonitis is the second leading infectious cause of death in cats. FIP has no known cure, and there is still much to be learned about this deadly disease. Once a cat is infected, he will die.

Cats become infected by inhaling or swallowing the virus, thought to be shed in the saliva, urine and feces of infected cats. Cats at the highest risk for the disease are those who are allowed outdoors, those raised in multiple-cat households and those stressed from infection, malnutrition or overcrowding. Very old and very young cats also seem to be affected more often.

The effusive, or "wet," form of the disease results in a progressive, painless swelling of the abdomen with fluid. Fluid may also accumulate

SPAYING OR NEUTERING

Your kitten should be spayed or neutered. Period.

Spaying or neutering (altering) refers to the surgical removal of an animal's reproductive organs. Despite Kitty's biological urges to the contrary, there are already too many kittens being born.

It's estimated that four kittens out of each litter of five will not find a good home. That warm, fuzzy wonder you're cuddling is the lucky fifth. Preventing the births of unwanted kittens is a moral obligation of responsible pet owners. Neutering also reduces and eliminates sexually related problem behaviors.

Because cats may become parents at as early as four months of age, the American Veterinary Medical Association now endorses neutering from 16 weeks on. Some shelters provide the services as early as 8 weeks of age. Young kittens bounce back from surgery more quickly than do older cats.

in the chest cavity, making breathing difficult. The non-effusive, or "dry," form of the disease causes incoordination, partial or complete paralysis of hind legs, convulsions, personality changes and eye disease. Some cats may have a combination of the wet and dry forms of FIP.

31

RESTRAINING YOUR KITTEN

Cats are escape artists, and if they don't want to be held, they will squirm right out of your hands. If you need to examine your kitten closely and he's not cooperating, try these techniques.

- For a somewhat cooperative kitten: Place one hand under your kitten's lower jaw with thumb on one side fingers on the other. Don't hold too tightly! Use your other hand to check your kitten. If there's someone to help you, you can use your other hand to hold one of Kitty's front paws while the other person examines him.

- If your kitten is uncooperative: If you're by yourself, grasp your kitten's fur behind the neck. This is what Mom did to immobilize Kitty if he had to be moved. If you have a helper, grasp the fur behind the neck and pick up a front paw.

Feline Immunodeficiency Virus (FIV)

Feline immunodeficiency virus belongs to the same family as the human immunodeficiency virus (HIV) that causes AIDS. The viruses are species specific, which means people cannot get the cat virus, and cats cannot be infected by the human disease.

FIV is most commonly transmitted through bites. Male cats and free-roaming outdoor cats are at the highest risk, although kittens can be exposed by their infected mother when she bites through the umbilical cord immediately after their birth.

Cats with the disease first show only vague symptoms like anemia or recurrent fever. As FIV progresses, cats begin to lose weight, develop enlarged lymph nodes and often suffer secondary illnesses, including upper respiratory infections, bladder and kidney infections and severe gum infections.

There is no treatment for this fatal disease, and currently no protective vaccinations are available. The only way to protect your kitten is to prevent exposure to other cats who might be infected.

Rabies

Caused by a virus that attacks the brain, rabies affects virtually all mammals, including humans, but today the cat is the most commonly infected pet in the United States.

Rabies is transmitted by direct animal-to-animal contact, usually through a bite. It generally takes three to eight weeks for symptoms to appear. Animals first stop eating and drinking and seek solitude. Then, they either show signs of paralysis or become vicious. Once symptoms develop, rabies is always fatal, and victims should be euthanized to avoid their suffering an agonizing death or infecting anyone else.

Lower Urinary Tract Disease (LUTD)

Lower urinary tract disease is actually a group of disorders with various causes that can result in serious urologic difficulties in cats. Adult cats are at the highest risk for LUTD, but older kittens can be affected.

The most serious condition is a blockage, caused by crystals and/or mucus, that prevents the cat from voiding urine. LUTD has been linked to diet and more recently to stress. Today virtually all commercial cat foods are formulated to reduce the risk of LUTD.

Warning signs include bloody urine, urine with a strong ammonia odor, squatting or straining, crying at the end of urination, listlessness, poor appetite and excessive thirst. A cat with a blockage must be seen immediately by a veterinarian. Coma and death will occur within 72 hours of complete obstruction.

33

This vet examines a kitten's eyes to see that they are bright and clear.

Check your kitty's paws to see if it's time to trim his claws.

HOME HEALTH EXAM

An important part of preventive care is to check your kitten regularly for signs of problems. These could include strange bumps, cuts, scabs, runny nose, discharge in the eyes, sneezing, drooling, swelling, hair loss, lethargy, irritability and incontinence—anything out of the ordinary.

Body Work

While you're petting or grooming your cat, move your fingertips all the way down to the skin and feel all over the body. You're feeling for lumps, scratches, rough spots, dry areas, inflammation or localized pain. Include his legs, feet and tail.

Pay particular attention to the head. Look at your cat's eyes. Are they shiny and clear? How about the ears? Are they pink and healthy looking with no waxy debris or dirt or foul odor? Is your cat's nose running? Try to push back the lips and examine the teeth. Are they white and whole or do you see tartar buildup or possibly a chipped tooth? Again, anything unusual should be passed along to your veterinarian for consultation.

Examine your cat's claws. Do they need trimming? (See chapter 5 for instructions on clipping nails.)

Don't forget to look at your cat's urogenital area. Do you notice any peculiar discharge, swelling, crusting or redness?

Last but not least, learn your cat's body language, preferences and habits. Cats are good at hiding signs of illness, and knowing what's normal for your cat will help you notice when something's off. Here are some signs to look for:

- Dull coat or scraggly appearance

- Excessive drinking

- Loss of appetite for up to three days

- Diarrhea for more than one day

- Trouble eliminating or inappropriate elimination

- Blood in the urine or feces

- Coughing, wheezing or excessive sneezing

- Sudden weight change (increase or decrease)

- Unusual discharge from eyes or nose

- Hair loss

- Sudden behavior change—unusually aggressive or passive

Anything unusual or worrisome warrants a call to your veterinarian. For emergencies, like bleeding or shock, see the section on emergencies and first aid later in this chapter.

INTESTINAL PARASITES

Roundworms

Nearly all kittens will have roundworms acquired from their mothers' milk, from contaminated soil, or from eating infected animals or insects. Severely infected kittens may have a potbellied appearance, a dull coat, diarrhea or mucus in the stool, and they may cough and lose their appetite. You may find spaghetti-like worms coiled in Kitty's stool or vomit.

Veterinary diagnosis is made by identifying eggs during microscopic examination of a stool sample. Many veterinarians recommend worming all kittens routinely for roundworms; two doses of a liquid oral medication usually are given two weeks apart.

Hookworms

Hookworms are a more serious parasite that can cause severe anemia. Signs include weight loss, diarrhea, vomiting, listlessness and lack of energy. In young kittens, hookworms can cause sudden collapse and death.

Cats are infected by ingesting eggs found in feces, and hookworm larvae are also able to penetrate the skin to infect a cat. Adult worms are tiny, less than one-half inch long,

No part of your kitten's body should go unexamined!

35

and can't be seen in the feces. Diagnosis is made by identifying eggs during microscopic examination of the stool. The same treatment for roundworms also eliminates hookworms.

Tapeworm

Tapeworms are the most common intestinal parasites seen in cats. Tapeworms require an intermediate host, the flea, for transmission. Cats become infected by grooming away and swallowing fleas.

Diagnosis is made when worm segments are found wiggling in the litter box, the anal area of the pet's fur or perhaps your kitten's favorite spot on the sofa. Dried segments look like grains of rice.

Diarrhea, and occasionally blood, is seen with tapeworms, and very large numbers can cause partial blockage. Pills or shots are available to eliminate infections, but the best prevention is flea control. Some veterinarians recommend tapeworm treatment for any cat with fleas.

Coccidia

Coccidia is a protozoal parasite that colonizes and attacks the lining of the intestine. Kittens and cats can be infected by coming into contact with an infected animal's stool or by eating infected rodents.

This tabby shows off his clean, healthy ears!

The signs may come and go, and they include bloody and loose stool with a lot of mucus. Diagnosis is made by microscopic examination of a stool sample. Your veterinarian will prescribe either a liquid or pill medication to eliminate the problem.

Giardia

Giardia is another type of protozoa, which infects the small intestine. Cats transmit giardia to each other through contact with feces, food or water. The parasite causes chronic diarrhea, and affected cats may also have a poor hair coat and a distended stomach from gas. Diagnosis is sometimes difficult, and giardia is best diagnosed and treated by your veterinarian.

OTHER PARASITES

Ear Mites

Ear mites are the most common cause of ear disease in cats and kittens. These tiny parasites may infest your kitten's ear and cause extreme irritation that can lead to infection. They crawl through the ear canal and bite the skin to feed on lymph.

YOUR KITTEN'S WELL-BEING

Equally important to the sound growth of your kitten is his mental health. Kittens are curious creatures and can be quite social when they want to be. Don't leave your kitten alone for the entire day—at least until he's settled in and knows you and what to expect. Keep a supply of toys on hand, and keep the litter box clean. And most of all, enjoy your kitten!

Affected kittens scratch their ears, shake their heads and often have a dark crumbly or tarry substance inside the ear. Left untreated, ear mites can progress to inflammation and infection. Your veterinarian will diagnose the problem and prescribe the appropriate treatment.

Heartworms

Heartworms are blood parasites that are transmitted by mosquitoes. They primarily affect dogs but can also infect cats. Heartworms interfere with blood circulation and heart function. Infected cats often show no signs, then suddenly collapse and die. Others vomit intermittently.

Outdoor, middle-aged cats are at the highest risk, but exposure can take place during kittenhood. To become infected, cats must live in an area where infected dogs provide microfilariae, and where mosquitoes have a taste for both cats and dogs. If heartworms are a problem for dogs in your area, medications are available from your veterinarian that will prevent your kitten from becoming infected.

Fleas

The top complaint of pet owners, fleas are more than mere itchy aggravations. They can transmit disease and cause severe allergic reactions.

Blood loss from fleas can kill your kitten. Signs include lethargy, reluctance to play and loss of appetite. See your veterinarian immediately if the normally pink areas around your kitten's eyes and ears become very pale. (See chapter 5 for advice on controlling fleas.)

SKIN PROBLEMS

Allergies

Allergies are the immune system's response to an irritant. These irritants can be as varied as pollen, hair spray, certain fabrics, dust or insect bites,

Many flea control products are gentle enough for young kittens and easy enough to apply at home.

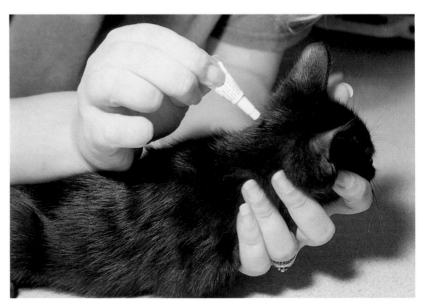

which cause swelling, sneezing, itching, closing of the eyelids, diarrhea or vomiting.

The irritating substances are called allergens, and they enter the system through the lungs, digestive tract, injection (a bug bite, for example) or simple skin exposure. As long as the cat continues to be exposed to the allergen, he will continue to have an allergic reaction. It is sometimes difficult to determine exactly what the allergen is. Cats with allergies suffer, and they must be taken to the veterinarian, who can perform tests to determine the source of the allergen and to prescribe a sufficient treatment.

Ringworm

Although several "worms" have already been discussed in this chapter, this one is not a parasite. Ringworm is a fungal infection that leaves a circle (ring) of hair loss and scaly skin. There is sometimes a red ring at the margin of the spot. Ringworm itself doesn't itch, but when the dry, scaly skin breaks into sores, it can cause itching. Ringworm is contagious between species, so any pet in the household can transmit it to another pet or to a person. If you

FIGHTING FLEAS

Remember that the fleas you see on your kitten are only part of the problem—the smallest part of the problem. To rid your kitten and home of fleas, you need to treat the animal and your home. Here's how:

Identify where your kitten(s) sleeps. These are "hot spots."

Clean your kitten's bedding regularly by vacuuming and washing.

Spray "hot spots" with a nontoxic, long-lasting flea larvicide.

If your kitten spends time outdoors, treat his favorite haunts ("hot spots") with insecticide.

Kill flea eggs on kittens with a product made specifically for kittens containing insect growth regulators (IGRs).

Consult your vet before treating Kitty.

notice a bald spot on your cat, you should have him checked for ringworm. Your veterinarian will prescribe treatment.

Feline Acne

Some cats develop pimple-like bumps or blackheads under their chins. This is feline acne, and it is more common in cats with oily skin. There are special shampoos and ointments to treat this condition.

EMERGENCIES AND FIRST AID

Emergencies may require first aid, but you should always follow home care immediately with veterinary attention. Gently wrap your injured kitten in a thick towel to prevent him from fighting you or further hurting himself. Place your ill or injured kitten in a box so that he can't see out; this will help calm him during the ride to the hospital.

Bleeding

Control bleeding by placing a gauze compress or clean washcloth directly on the wound and applying pressure. If the blood soaks through, don't change the cloth; simply place a second compress or washcloth over the first one, and continue applying the pressure.

Burns

Apply cold water for five minutes to burns. If you're unable to immerse the burned area, soak a washcloth in ice water, wring it out and lightly apply to the burned area. Treat chemical

There's no telling where your unpredictable, inquisitive kitten could end up; so it is important to know first-aid basics—just in case.

burns, such as those caused by caustic household cleaners, by flushing with cool water for five minutes or longer.

Respiratory Difficulty

A kitten may stop breathing due to electrocution, drowning, strangulation or choking. If you suspect a foreign object and can readily see it when you open his mouth, you can try to remove it with tweezers. You should never pull string from your kitten's mouth; it may have a needle or fishhook on the end. Leave that one for your veterinarian.

Drowning

For cases of drowning, grasp the kitten's hind legs with one hand and the nape of his neck with the other, and turn him upside down. Give him several brisk shakes or even several rapid downward swings, to help expel water from his lungs.

Resuscitation

If your kitten still doesn't breathe, place him on one side on a table or flat sturdy surface. Find the "elbow" of the front leg, and place your first

FIRST-AID FOR CATS

Emergencies are the kinds of situations you hope never occur, but for which you should be most prepared. Keep the following items together, along with the name and phone number of your veterinarian and emergency clinic, so you can be prepared should your cat need emergency care:

adhesive tape

antibiotic ointment

blanket

cardboard box

cotton (balls, swabs, wrap)

hydrogen peroxide (3 percent)

oil (vegetable or mineral)

soap

thermometer (digital)

tweezers

washcloth

three fingers flat on his side, behind the elbow. Press firmly, then release quickly; repeat every five seconds until he breathes on his own.

If the lungs are injured, you may need to breathe air into your kitten's lungs. Place him on his tummy, with his head in an upright position. Keeping his lips closed, place your lips over his nose and gently blow for two to three seconds. Repeat every two

Remember to keep your kitten's well-being first on your priority list. Cuddle with him, socialize him and make his home safe and comfortable.

42

seconds. Continue artificial respiration until your kitten begins breathing on his own. As long as his heart still beats (you'll feel the pulse on his side behind the left elbow) continue trying, even up to 30 minutes.

Topical Poison

The most common poisoning occurs from misapplication of flea products. Poisoned kittens salivate, tremble, act dazed or may even lose consciousness. Signs can be immediate or can occur several hours after the flea product application.

As soon as you see the signs, rinse your kitten with clear, cool water. Use a plain shampoo that doesn't have insecticide to wash the poison off. Then wrap your kitten in a towel and get him to the veterinarian.

Other Poisons

Your kitten's curiosity can get him in all kinds of trouble, and swallowing any number of common household products can poison him. Many human medications, such as aspirin and Tylenol, are poisonous to cats; chocolate is also deadly; and certain houseplants can burn his mouth and make him sick.

Antifreeze tastes sweet but destroys kidney function if your kitten drinks it. Bug bites and stings can turn from itchy irritations to deadly reactions. Signs of toxicity vary depending on what Kitty gets into but may include diarrhea, vomiting, incoordination, convulsions or breathing trouble.

Treatment also depends on the poison and ranges from inducing vomiting to feeding your kitten something to neutralize the agent. Unless you are very far from help, don't attempt home remedies, but simply get your poisoned pet to the veterinarian. Take the poison

POISON ALERT

If your cat has ingested a potentially poisonous substance, waste no time. Call the National Animal Poison Control Center hot line:

(800) 548-2423 ($30 per case) or

(900) 680-0000 ($20 first five minutes; $2.95 each additional minute)

package and a sample of your kitten's vomit with you to help the doctor determine the best treatment.

CHAPTER FOUR

Positively Nutritious

Whether your kitten is destined to be a finicky feline or a gourmet glutton, mealtimes will be major events in her life. Kittens depend on good nutrition, not only to fuel their daily play, but also to ensure they grow up healthy and stay that way.

NUTRITIONAL NEEDS

Nutrients are the substances in food that provide nourishment. Cats require a combination of six different classes of nutrients for good health: water, protein, carbohydrates, lipids (fats), minerals and vitamins.

This calico cat requires fewer calories than her rapidly growing baby does.

45

Feeding Life Stages

Kittens have different nutritional needs than do adult cats. Growing kittens require more protein, fat, calcium, phosphorus, magnesium, vitamin A and vitamin D than do mature felines. The AAFCO has established nutritional guidelines for each life stage that cat foods must meet to be able to label the product "complete and balanced." Life stages are defined as growth and reproduction (for kittens and pregnant or nursing mothers), maintenance (adult cats) or all life stages (kittenhood, motherhood and adult).

Professional breeders consider a cat to be a kitten until she's nine months old, but some cats continue growing after that. Your cat should remain on kitten formula for as long as she's growing, for at least a year. Then, switch Kitty to adult rations. Kitten food contains more calories than adult food does, and a cat who has stopped growing can become overweight if she continues eating kitten food.

This is hard work, isn't it? Well, you can rest assured that all major

TUNA FISH

Cats find the strong fishy smell of tuna very appealing, tempting owners to feed it as a special treat or a preferred diet. However, feeding a cat a lot of tuna fish can cause steatitis, a condition where vitamin E is destroyed by the excessive amounts of fatty acids in the food. Another potential problem is that the cat may decide it wants a tuna fish–only diet and will turn her nose up at regular cat food. Prevent these problems by feeding only very small amounts of tuna sporadically, as a treat. Make sure it is packed in water, not oil.

Fresh, cool water is essential for your kitten.

manufacturers of cat food will meet your strict criteria. Now you only need to choose the brand.

TYPES OF FOOD

Cat foods generally come in both dry and canned forms. Some kittens may have distinct preferences, while others may be easy to please.

Dry food is relatively inexpensive, storable without refrigeration and very convenient to use. Dry cat food remains palatable and nutritious for up to 12 months, even after the bag has been opened. Dry foods are more likely to decrease the rate of tartar accumulation on kitty teeth.

Canned varieties are a little more expensive but extremely palatable, and they have high caloric density. They come in a variety of flavors. Canned food must be refrigerated after opening. It contains about 70 percent moisture, which will partially fulfill your kitten's need for water. Unopened canned cat food will last nearly indefinitely, but most manufacturers recommend using canned products within two years.

Semi-moist foods are packaged as individual servings and are convenient travel food, but they aren't appropriate for everyday use. They are kept moist by ingredients like corn syrup that bind water and prevent the food from drying out. It's quite palatable, but the binding ingredient may cause your kitten to need to drink more water.

SCHEDULING MEALS

Your kitten should be fed in the same place every day, and a bowl of clean, fresh water must be available at all times. Put Kitty's food station some distance from her bathroom facilities to avoid bruising sensitive feline sensibilities. Usually, a low-traffic end of the kitchen or laundry room works well. Each pet should have her own food bowl set some distance from the others.

READING THE CAT FOOD LABEL

Cats, like people, have certain specific nutritional requirements. For the most part, how well the different cat foods meet these needs has been ascertained through extensive testing by regulatory organizations, most notably the Association of American Feed Control Officials (AAFCO). When choosing a food for your cat, look for this type of statement on the label: "Animal feeding tests using AAFCO procedures." These foods were tested on cats.

When reviewing ingredients, remember they're listed in decreasing order by weight, which means the heavier, more abundant ingredients will be first. These include meats (or fish) and water. Remember, too, that cats are carnivores and must eat meat. They do not do well on a vegetarian diet. Ask your veterinarian or a cat breeder for dietary recommendations.

47

This nursing mama cat eats a food specifically fit for the nutritional needs of the motherhood stage of life.

This kitten seems overwhelmed by the feast in front of her.

FREE-FEEDING

Most cats fed free-choice eat every few hours all day long, but they consume the same amount each day. Some adult cats don't know when to quit, and they will continue to eat as long as the bowl is full. However, obesity is not a problem in kittens, who need every mouthful of food they can get. Free-choice feeding works particularly well with growing kittens, who may not be able to eat enough in one serving to sustain them throughout a hard day's play.

Canned food spoils if left sitting in a bowl all day long, so it must be scheduled as meals. Measure the daily amount needed, divide it by three or four meals and offer the food at the same times each day. Alternatively, set out a bit more food than the entire daily amount, and allow Kitty to eat for up to 30 minutes; then pick up the bowl and put it back in the refrigerator until the next meal.

Probably the best method for kittens is a combination of free-choice and scheduled meals. Kittens younger than 10 weeks old may have trouble with dry food. Feed canned food or kitten kibble moistened with warm water (1 ounce water to 1^1/$_2$ cups food) until your baby is aggressively eating the diet. Set moistened dry food down three to four times a day, slowly reducing the amount of water until your kitten reaches 10 weeks of age. Then you can leave dry food out all day.

Even if dry food is available at all times, you may wish to offer a spoonful or two of canned food in the morning and evening as a special treat. Be sure to pick it up after half an hour so that your kitten doesn't consume spoiled food and get a tummy ache. Cats prefer their food at room or body temperature, so a couple of seconds in the microwave will make refrigerated food more palatable. Eating cold food may cause your kitten to spit up, which may not bother her, but it will stain the carpet.

ABOUT MILK

Although milk is an excellent food source, it should never replace your kitten's water. Also, cow's milk and cat's milk contain different proteins. Some kittens past weaning don't have enough of the enzyme lactase to digest the milk sugar

GOOD AND BAD SNACKS

Besides feeding a high-quality commercial cat food, you can feed your cat some people foods—occasionally, and always as part of the cat's regular diet. Always consider total caloric intake. If you're going to treat Kitty, reduce her regular meal somewhat. Be careful what you give as treats. Here are some good ones (+) and bad ones (−):

+ Vegetables, raw or cooked, without sauce

+ Broth from water-packed meat and fish

+ Cooked meat (poultry, beef, lamb, pork, liver), with all bones removed

+ Cheese or yogurt

+ Fresh fruit

− Raw fish

− Uncooked meat

− Dog food

− Bones of any kind

− Chocolate in any form

− Candies, desserts, sweets

− Onions and raw potatoes

49

lactose, and the result is diarrhea. That's no fun for you, your kitten or the carpet. It's best to avoid cow's

GRASS FOR YOUR CAT

Cats crave the nutrients in grass, and wheat grass is especially beneficial for your feline. You can grow a patch of wheat grass at home and make it available to your cat. Buy organic hard wheat berries at a health food store. You'll need about 1 tablespoon per crop. Soak the wheat berries overnight in water, then drain and allow the berries to dry on a piece of paper towel. In a ceramic bowl, place approximately 1 inch of potting soil, and plant the berries in it. Spray the soil with water, and then cover the layer of wheat berry seeds with 1/4 inch of peat moss or more soil. Place in a bright area. Keep moist, and avoid overwatering or the crop will get moldy. The grass should be ready for your cat in a week or 10 days.

milk and just stick to commercial kitten food.

The more you learn about feline nutrition, the better the care you'll provide for your kitten. Don't leave the decision up to Kitty; after all, she'd probably prefer crunching crickets and munching mice.

KEEPING KITTY SLIM

As they age, cats—especially indoor cats—are prone to weight problems. This is because they exercise less and their metabolisms slow down, just like ours.

If you notice your cat's stomach area getting round and you have a hard time feeling the ribs through the flesh, your cat already is or is

A new kitty litter pan has been converted into a garden of edible grass.

getting fat. Consult with your veterinarian first to determine how bad the problem is and second to discuss dietary changes. There are a number of "lite" cat foods on the market, and your veterinarian can assist you in choosing one. These foods contain more fiber and less fat so they fill your cat up without filling her out.

Exercise is essential for all cats, and you don't need a feline fitness center to keep kitty in top shape. You will need to make a point of playing with your cat every day.

This young man plays with his kittens to help keep them trim and fit.

51

CHAPTER FIVE

Pretty Kitty

No doubt you've seen your feline neatnik washing his whiskers. In fact, adult cats spend up to 50 percent of their awake time grooming themselves. Hygiene is learned early, and kittens who aren't well cared for by Momma-cat frequently develop into unkempt adults. By the time kittens are two weeks old, they begin to lick themselves. Most kittens learn grooming techniques before they leave their mom, and they use their tongues, teeth and dampened forepaws and hind claws as kitty wash rags and scratching/combing tools.

Despite your kitten's dedication to self-grooming, he'll need help cleaning those hard-to-reach places. Longhair cats require more care than do shorthair kitties. Regular grooming helps reduce the amount

of shed hair and keep hairballs from forming.

Dry indoor heat stimulates house cats to shed most of the time, and only the removal of loose hair will keep longhair kitty coats unmatted. A matted coat is not only painful for the cat when it pulls tender skin, but it also provides a perfect flea environment.

Grooming is a wonderful opportunity to examine your kitten for unusual lumps and bumps; ear, eye or claw problems; and parasites or skin problems. It also helps strengthen the bond between you and your pet. To your kitten, grooming just plain feels good and is a way of expressing affection.

Weekly grooming will keep most kitty coats in fine form.

your knees, and set Kitty on top. Use a white sheet so it's easier to tell if debris that has fallen from your cat's coat is just dirt or is something problematic.

CLEANING YOUR KITTEN

Regular brushing and combing takes only five minutes or so. But be warned: Kitty may get addicted to the wonderful attention, in which case it will be impossible to groom him too much.

Cats thrive on routine, so set aside a special time and place for grooming, and stick to the schedule. To begin, spread a white sheet or towel on a table, or on the floor between

Start with Petting

Always start with petting. Get Kitty's motor rumbling by running your fingers through his fur. Not only will he enjoy the attention, but you'll find mats or burrs ahead of time and avoid a painful ripping encounter with the comb or brush. Finger-combing also familiarizes you with the angles and planes of your cat's body. Running a comb rudely across a bony spine or into tender nipples

53

ROUTINE GROOMING

These are the things you should do at least once a week to keep your kitten looking and feeling his best:

Brush Kitty.

Comb Kitty.

Check skin, eyes, ears and paws for problem spots.

Clip nails.

Check teeth and gums.

Play with Kitty afterwards.

will aggravate Kitty, who will abruptly cut the session short.

ESTABLISH A PATTERN

Some groomers begin with the tail and flanks, then work their way forward to the sides, tummy, neck and face. Others reverse the procedure. Establish your own routine, as long as you cover the whole cat. Start and end each session grooming the part of your kitten he particularly enjoys, like his throat or cheeks.

Get your kitten used to the equipment by letting him sniff and investigate or even play with the comb or brush.

LET KITTY BE YOUR GUIDE

Think of scratching the skin rather than combing the fur, and make grooming an extension of petting. Let the kitten be your guide. It's better if your kitten asks for more rather than complains when you've gone too far.

At first, keep grooming sessions to only a minute or two, and stop before your cat demands you to; then finish later. By continuing to groom a reluctant cat, you reinforce his discomfort and turn the whole experience into one he dreads rather than one he looks forward to. You want grooming to be fun. Finish each session with a favorite game.

MESSY MATS

Longhairs typically mat behind the ears, under the chin and in the armpits of all four legs. Some also get nasty mats in their "britches," beneath the tail where feces or litter may catch.

Never use scissors to cut out a mat. You run the risk of cutting the thin, tender skin as your kitten squirms. Instead, use a wide-toothed comb and start from the hair tips at the end of the mat; then work progressively deeper and deeper. Rub a bit of cornstarch into the mat to help untangle the fur, then comb again. Try threading the wide-tooth comb through the mat to prevent painful pulling; then brush over it with your slicker brush. If all else fails, use an electric razor to break up the mat. You may need a professional groomer's help.

Regular grooming should prevent embarrassing and painful mats from developing. A thorough combing and the removal of mats are a must before bathing; otherwise, the water will make the mats as hard as cement, and to remove them, you will have to shave them off.

IF YOUR KITTEN HAS FLEAS

After combing or brushing your kitten, examine the white-cloth grooming surface. So-called "flea dirt" looks like black dots and will be caught by the towel, alerting you that parasites have moved in, which means Kitty needs a flea treatment.

Particular care must be taken with kittens when treating them for fleas, because the insecticides that poison the bugs can also kill your kitten. Cats are more susceptible to insecticides than dogs are, and kittens

are the most sensitive of all. Safe products are available from pet stores and from your veterinarian, but you must read the label and follow all the directions. Only use products that actually say "safe for kittens." Even some of the so-called "natural" citrus-based products with d-limonene can be toxic to your kitten.

Comb Them Out

For controlling fleas on your kitten, a flea comb is the safest way to go. The narrow teeth catch and comb the bugs out. Prepare a bowl of soapy water, and comb your kitten with short strokes. Dip the comb in the water to drown the caught fleas.

The next-safest route is to use products containing pyrethrin,

Flea combs can be incorporated into regular grooming sessions to check for fleas and "flea dirt."

HAIRBALLS

To cats, grooming is a way of life. They are clean creatures who use their specially designed tongues to both keep their hair and skin debris-free and to cover themselves with scent. Hairballs are accumulations of the loose fur that the cat swallows as he grooms. This fur either travels through the cat's digestive system and is defecated or irritates the system and is vomited out.

You can help keep hairballs to a minimum by combing out your cat's loose hair. If he becomes constipated anyway, you can put a small amount of petroleum jelly on his paws to lick off (cats like the taste). But with regular combing from you and regular grooming by them, cats can handle their hairballs naturally. Anything unusual should be reported to your veterinarian.

which is probably the least toxic insecticide available for use on kittens. With your veterinarian's approval, use a shampoo for an initial flea kill. Between baths, use a kitten-safe spray. Spray the product on a cotton ball, and first wipe it carefully around the face and neck, then over the body.

You must also treat your kitten's environment to keep new buggy hitchhikers from catching a ride.

BATHING YOUR KITTEN

Kittens should not be bathed until they are at least four weeks old. Younger kittens have trouble regulating their temperature and can easily be chilled and develop pneumonia. For touch-ups and spot cleaning between baths, commercial waterless cat shampoos are available that don't require rinsing. Pour the product on a soft cloth, rub it into the coat and then comb it out. The kitten is never submerged and feels like he's being stroked.

Sometimes, nothing will suffice but an all-out dunking. There are three basic cat-bathing methods: the shower, the pan and the bucket. No matter which technique you choose, get everything ready before introducing Kitty to the idea.

Prepping the Place

The room should be warm and draft-free. Get all the breakables and scary stuff like shower curtains put away or looped out of reach. You'll need a washcloth for Kitty's face, two or more dry towels and kitten shampoo at the ready.

Run the water before you bring in the victim . . . er, your kitten. The water should be kitten-temperature, about 102°F.

The Shower Method—Place a towel or rubber mat in the bottom of the sink for a foothold. While keeping one hand on your kitten, use a handheld spray attachment to wet his fur thoroughly, avoiding his face. Holding the nozzle against his body is less upsetting to your kitten.

Never spray your kitten in the face; you wouldn't like it and neither will he. Use a washcloth to wet and wash the face, and avoid getting soap in his eyes, mouth, nose or ears. You want to make the experience as positive and stress-free as possible.

Talk to your kitten soothingly, or perhaps play soft music to help calm him. Flea shampoos should be applied around the kitten's neck first, to make a sudsy barrier that prevents fleas from hiding in the ears and facial fur. Lather Kitty's body, legs, feet and tail. If the shampoo is for fleas, the lather must set for up to 10 minutes.

Stay with your kitten to make sure a sudsy projectile doesn't escape the sink and get soapsuds on the floor. Try wrapping your bubbly kitty in a towel, and hold him for the prescribed time. Then rinse him, using the wash rag to eliminate shampoo from his face. Feed water gently onto his fur, starting at the neck and letting it sluice suds off the

This kitty doesn't mind water and suds as long as his face stays dry.

fur. Once you're sure all the soap is gone, rinse him one more time; any shampoo left will dry out the coat and skin and cause dandruff.

The Bucket/Pan Methods—For kittens who are upset by spraying water, the bucket or pan method may be less stressful.

Fill two or three containers with kitten-temperature water. The water level should reach your kitten's neck as he stands on his hind legs and clutches the side of the container.

Grasp your kitten beneath the chest with one hand, while supporting his furry bottom in the other, and slowly lower him in the first basin of water. Avoid splashing,

since that's what upsets cats the most.

Continue supporting the kitten's chest as you work the water into his coat with your other hand. Lift out the kitten and set him in the tub (or on the towel or drip-pan on the counter); then add shampoo and suds him up. Use a washcloth on his face.

Dip the scrubbed, sudsy kitten back into the first container, still supporting his chest, and rinse him thoroughly. Lift him out, and use your free hand to squeegee water off his fur. Then, repeat the dip-and-squeegee process in the second bucket or sink, and again in the third. Rinse his face with the washcloth.

Warm air from a blow dryer on a gentle setting will help dry Kitty quickly and thoroughly.

Finishing Touches

Finally, wrap your kitten in a warm, dry towel and blot up as much water as possible. Kittens catch cold easily and must be kept warm until completely dry. Shorthair kitties dry quickly, but longer fur can take several hours and may need the help of a blow dryer. Use only the lowest setting, or it can get too hot and burn tender kitten skin.

DENTAL HYGIENE

Just like human teeth, cat teeth that aren't properly cared for get dirty, cause gum disease and bad breath, and can ultimately decay and abscess, causing much pain. Start regular teeth cleaning now, once or twice weekly, to get your kitten used to the routine.

At about five months of age, he will have most of his permanent teeth. Do not brush them with people toothpaste; it can upset his stomach. Use plain water or a special commercial cat toothpaste.

Using a very soft baby toothbrush or a piece of gauze wrapped around your finger, massage his teeth and gums in a circular motion. Cleaning the outside of the teeth is the most

Start checking your kitten's mouth regularly (and gently) to get him used to it.

helpful, since he uses his tongue to clean the inside. Keep sessions short.

EYE CARE

Kittens with flatter faces, like Persian-type breeds, have prominent eyes that tend to tear. This can lead to a cosmetic problem if the tears stain the fur beneath the eyes of light-faced kittens.

The problem can also be more serious: If not gently cleaned away, the normal secretions can dry on the fur and cause the eyes and lids to become inflamed or even infected. Tears should be clear and liquid, not thick or dark-colored, both of which indicate illness.

PAWS THAT CLAW: NAIL CARE

When your kitten walks, his claws rarely touch the ground, and he does not wear them down naturally even by using the scratching post. Overgrown claws can split, break off and bleed, or they can tear when caught by carpeting or furniture. Claw maintenance prevents problems from happening.

The best time to start claw maintenance is before your kitten actually needs it. With a tiny kitten, simply go through the motions to get Kitty used to having his paws handled. On young kittens, human nail clippers work fine, and there are also clippers available at pet stores or veterinary offices.

Cat claws are like human fingernails and are made of dead protein that has no nerves and, therefore, no feeling. The nerves are in the quick, inside the claw at the root, which shows through pink. Never cut into the pink portion because it is very tender and can bleed. Clip off only the curved white or clear tip of the claw.

Gently wipe out the corners of the kitten's eyes with cotton balls soaked with saline. Daily attention will help prevent staining. Pet stores also have kitten-safe products for removing the stain.

EAR CARE

Examine your kitten's ears every week. The inside should be pink and relatively clean; a small amount of honey-colored wax is normal. If the wax is very thick or dark and crumbly, your kitten may have parasites, which must be treated by your veterinarian.

For normal maintenance, use an ear-cleaning solution available from your veterinarian or pet store, or a bit of baby oil. Don't put anything inside the ear; simply swab the visible portion with a cotton ball soaked with the solution. You can also carefully use cotton swabs to clean all the little crevices, but be cautious. You risk damaging the ears if you probe too far down.

CHAPTER SIX

Cat Characteristics

As you walk by, Kamikaze Kitten darts from beneath the sofa and grapples with your shoelaces. Then, in an eye blink, she's stalking imaginary prey, intent upon ambushing the malevolent creature stirring behind the drapes. But before she reaches her goal, something else distracts her. Now your kitten is bouncing through the room like a puppet on springs.

Oh, what fun we have watching kittens play. As soon as they can wobble about on unsteady paws, they're bopping each other's ears and trying to catch their own (and Mom's) tail.

But to your kitten, these games are more than furry fun.

Cats start playing at four weeks of age, and the games continue their whole life long. Play helps youngsters practice and develop the skills they'll need to be successful adults. Games also teach kittens important lessons about their world and promote physical and social development.

These wrestle maniacs don't know it, but their playtime together helps to keep them toned and develops social skills.

THE GAME OF LIFE

Your kitten's senses are fully developed by about five weeks of age, but it takes longer to coordinate all those clumsy paws. Play helps develop the motor skills she'll use in everyday activities.

The first play behavior a kitten practices is on her back, belly up with paws waving in the air. As she

Every kitten game mimics an adult behavior used in hunting, fighting or mating.

grapples with that fluttering feather, she's also learning to coordinate claws and bites. This is a defensive pose adult cats use to bring all their claws into play.

Wrestling not only tones their muscles and perfects their biting and clawing techniques, it also teaches social skills. Youngsters learn proper feline etiquette and how to interact with both siblings and adults, like their mother. Exuberant kittens soon realize that claws hurt and that those uninhibited bites on Mom's tail result in a hiss and a swat.

The sideways shuffle, back arched high as they tiptoe around other kittens or objects, is used in defensive situations by adults.

Other play behavior includes the mouse pounce, bird swat, fish scoop,

Games express Kitty's curiosity and provide an outlet for exploration.

63

boxer stance and horizontal leaps. Games of tag or hide-and-seek echo the stalk, chase and pursuit used in hunting. Playing is also a fun way

THE SLEEPY KITTEN

You may have noticed that Kitty likes napping almost as much as playing. Kittens need more rest than adults do, but even grownup cats sleep about 16 hours every day. By the time Kitty is six years old, she will have spent only two years awake.

No one is sure why cats sleep so much. It may have to do with conserving energy so that awake time is spent in bursts of activity. In the wild, hunters who are extremely successful and catch mice quickly have more time to nap.

for your kitten to learn about objects. She discovers that a batting paw sends a ball or pencil rolling and bouncing across the floor, but that a bopped shoe just sits there. Play teaches her that a toy mouse stays put while she naps, but that a moth flutters away and hides.

Even more, play is a creative expression of your kitten's emotions. As your kitten grows up, she's very aware of the difference between play and serious business, even though the same skills are needed. Kittens and cats play because it's just plain fun.

INTERACTIVE PLAY

Playing with your kitten cements the bond of love and trust between you. Those who play together stay together. In effect, your kitten looks

There's no place a kitten can't sleep.

Everything that moves is fair game for kittens, even toes!

upon you as a "Super Cat," who supplies food, grooming and fun times, just like Momma-cat did.

Kittens want something to chase and capture that can be bitten, clawed and "killed." Your wiggling fingers are enticing, but don't encourage hand and finger games or your kitten will inevitably get in trouble when she draws blood. Besides, what's cute in a kitten becomes downright dangerous in a full-grown cat.

VARIATIONS OF TOYS

Light, easy-to-move-and-bite toys get raves from feline critics. Fishing-pole-style toys provide great interactive games. Movement that crosses her line of vision horizontally stimulates her chasing reaction more quickly than does movement directly away from her. Try rolling an object in front of your baby, and watch the fun. Some kittens even enjoy games of fetch.

Homemade toys are less expensive but provide just as much fun. An empty paper bag or box, a wad of crinkly paper or even the beam of a flashlight will delight your kitten. Try dropping a walnut inside an empty tissue box, and watch your kitten "fish."

Kittens often invent games that satisfy their curiosity. They learn to open cupboard doors, shred the hanging plant and climb the drapes. Just as with any baby, playtime should be supervised.

WHISKER-LICKING CLEAN

Your kitten's instinct to wash herself accomplishes more than just clean whiskers. Cats often groom when frightened, tense or hesitant about how to react to puzzling situations. Self-grooming may help the cat relieve tension and cope with conflict; the self-induced "kitty massage" seems to calm your kitten down. When your kitten is in a conflict or a stressful situation, she may seem ready to react, but instead suddenly stops and starts grooming herself.

Mutual Grooming

Mutual grooming begins when kittens start licking and grooming each other and their mother at about three weeks of age. Mutual grooming focuses on hard-to-reach places like the head.

But mutual grooming is primarily a social gesture rather than a hygienic

66

These kittens express their love and companionship.

one. Family cats often indulge in mutual grooming sessions, and they may purr and play with each other at the same time.

Cats extend this behavior to humans by licking us and accepting our petting. So when your kitten thinks enough of you to groom your hair, return the compliment. After all, the payment will be in whisker kisses and purrs.

KITTEN TALK

A kitten's vocabulary is a combination of both verbal and nonverbal language. Understanding what Kitty's trying to say will help you avoid misunderstandings and improve your relationship with your cat.

Some cats, like Siamese, are more vocal than others, but every cat has something to say. More than 16 different feline voice patterns have been identified, which are commonly divided in four categories: murmur patterns, vowel patterns, articulated sounds and strained intensity sounds.

Murmur Patterns

Murmur patterns include purrs and trills. These are the happy sounds

PURRS AND HISSES

Purring is normally associated with pleasure, but cats also purr when they're injured or distressed. Purring is a primal response, and kittens start doing it when they're just a few days old.

What causes purring? When stimulated, the brain sends signals to muscles in the throat and vocal cords to vibrate. The action of these muscles causes the purring sound and sensation.

Hissing, on the other hand, is a clear signal from the cat to steer clear! It's a sound meant to scare an intruder. In the act of hissing, a jet of air, as well as spit and sound, is shot out through the cat's mouth. The question is, who hissed first, the cat or the snake?

your kitten makes when she's feeling friendly and relaxed. Purrs range from quiet, almost silent vibrations, to reverberating rumbles that nearly rattle the windowpanes. Trills express joy when Kitty's bowl is filled or when you bring out a favorite toy.

Vowel Patterns

Vowel patterns, like meows, are feline demands for something. Meows vary from short, muted mews to raucous, multisyllabic catcalls. Kittens meow to Momma-cat, but otherwise meows seem aimed primarily at humans. Higher pitches generally have a more pleasant connotation, while the lower tones tend to indicate more agitation. Your kitten typically meows to be petted, for attention or more food and (if she's allowed) to go in and out.

Articulated Sounds

Articulated sounds like chirping and chattering usually indicate frustration. If you hear your kitten chittering, chances are she's seen something she can't reach—like a squirrel out the window.

Kittens (and cats) hiss when they sense danger.

Strained Intensity Sounds

Strained intensity sounds are used in mating, offense and defense. A frightened kitten may hiss and spit; an angry kitten may growl; and a defensive kitten howls, yowls, and finally, screams.

BODY LANGUAGE

Most cat language is nonverbal. Body language is second nature to cats, who are extremely visual animals. Experts speculate that silent "felinese" developed in wild cats as a way to communicate without alerting enemies or prey to their presence. Your kitten speaks volumes using tail twitches, ear flicks, eye winks and even fur and body positions.

Tails

The tail is probably the best communicator Kitty has, and it is a good indicator of her mood. An upright tail belongs to a confident cat checking her surroundings. An upright tail with a hook on the end is a friendly greeting to older cats and humans.

A tail in a relaxed horizontal position indicates a mellow mood, while a slightly curved and raised tail shows interest. But if your kitten reverses that curve so her tail becomes an arch, she's feeling threatened.

A wagging tail expresses aggravation. A twitch or two of the tip is a warning, which soon escalates to thumps and then to full lashing. A flailing tail says, "Lay off!" If you ignore the warning, Kitty will land an angry claw swipe, or worse.

Eyes

Feline eyes are windows to your kitten's soul. Curious, alert kittens are wide-eyed so that they won't miss a thing. Unblinking stares or slitted eyes are signs of aggression. Relaxed, trusting kittens let their eyelids droop as though sleepy.

Sudden emotion of any kind, from joy to fear or anger, is shown by sudden dilation of the pupils. Abrupt contraction of the pupils to a slit can warn of an imminent attack.

Ears

Kitten ears are equally expressive. When the ears are upright and the face is forward to catch every sound,

Kitty is interested and alert. Uneasy ears turn sideways like little airplane wings. Scaredy-cats press their ears flat to the side of the head. The more the back of the ear shows, the more ready the cat is to attack.

Fur and Whiskers

Even your kitten's fur signals mood and intention. Forward-facing whiskers mean that she's alert and checking things out. Spread whiskers show Kitty's happy and relaxed, but whiskers flattened against cheeks show she's fearful or plans to attack. Kittens aroused by strong emotion, such as fear or even play, fluff their fur and bristle their tails.

This kitten has wrapped her tail around herself, telling us she is cool, confident and content.

69

FELINE ACTORS

Despite all the bristled fur, flailing tails and hissing contests, cats are not great attackers. They're simply brilliant at posturing, and they use felinese to fake out their opponents without ever mussing a whisker.

A fearful cat bluffs her foe by trying to look bigger than she really is. She fluffs her fur and turns broadside, and she tiptoes sideways away from the threat, pressing her ears lower and lower. She spits, snarls and may try to warn away her enemy with a claw swipe. But if the enemy isn't impressed, she admits defeat and runs.

Even confident cats first try to frighten interlopers away. If a head-on, wide-eyed stare doesn't work, her ears turn to the side, her tail starts swinging, and she bares her teeth and lowers her head. Unless the intruder takes to her heels, a cat on the offensive will attack with tooth and claw.

Although cats do occasionally indulge in pitched battles, most avoid conflict by acting tougher than they really are. Posturing displays may go on for 20 minutes or longer, with both cats indulging in dancelike maneuvering involving fluffed fur and ferocious expressions and vocalizations. The victory belongs to the most dominant kitty, who doesn't lose face and slink away.

Body Position

Body position is a form of long-distance communication that displays kitty moods. A contented kitten typically sits on her haunches with her tail wrapped about herself. Dropping into a curtsy with front feet lowered and tail-end raised or rolling on the ground in front of you, is an invitation to play.

Confident kittens face threats head-on, while the uneasy kitten crouches with front paws drawn close to her chest. A fearful kitten turns into a Halloween cat, arching her back sideways to the enemy in order to look bigger and more impressive.

CHAPTER SEVEN

A Matter of Fact

IN THE BEGINNING

Cats got their start long before humans were on the scene. Miacids, the earliest forebear of modern cats, evolved during the mid-Paleocene epoch about 61 million years ago. The earliest Miacids were small but ferocious carnivores that lived in forests and probably looked something like today's shrews. Experts believe they were equally at home on the ground or climbing trees, and they probably had retractable claws, like modern kitties.

A variety of catlike creatures sprang from the pint-size Miacids and flourished throughout most of the world. Miacids became the founding fathers for all modern

72

Cats purred their way into human hearts many thousands of years ago, and they have been enriching our lives ever since.

carnivores, including the bear, weasel, badger, hyena, civet, genet, mongoose, raccoon, dog, fox, wolf and, of course, the entire cat family.

But cats didn't start looking much like cats until about 12 million years ago when creatures resembling today's felines first prowled and growled across the world. Nine million years later, the Felidae family tree branched into the major cat types we currently recognize, and all

modern-day cats, both big and small, evolved from these first felines.

Panthera are the big roaring cats: the lions, tigers, leopards and jaguars. Two big cats are so unique that they have their own genus: Acinonyx for the cheetah and Neofelis for the clouded leopard. Felis embraces more than 28 kinds of small cats, including cougars, bobcats, 23 subspecies of wildcats, and domestic cats like your kitten.

CAT MEETS HUMAN

Cats of all sizes were already on the scene when humans first appeared. People probably competed with cats for food, and no doubt they sometimes even stalked each other. Early humans envied the feline's success, and they celebrated the cat's hunting prowess in prehistoric cave drawings of lions. Cat amulets indicate that feline cults glorified the cat in Egypt as early as the 6th Dynasty.

Exactly when cats stepped over the threshold and became domesticated is still open to debate. Some experts believe domestication may have begun as early as 8,000 years ago. They point to a cat's jawbone dated 6000 B.C. discovered at an excavation site in southern Cyprus in 1983. Because this island has no native wild cats, it's believed the ancient kitty was brought there by human settlers.

Domestication

It's more generally accepted that cats were domesticated between 3,500 and 4,500 years ago in ancient Egypt. The first historical documents mentioning cats date from Egypt in 1668 B.C., and paintings of cats with collars

THE FIRST CAT

There are a number of different legends that explain how cats made their entrance into the world. According to Hebrew folklore, Noah was concerned that rats might be a problem on the ark, eating all the provisions, and he prayed to God for help. God responded by causing the lion, who was sleeping, to unleash a giant sneeze from which emerged a little cat.

In an Arabic legend, Noah's sons and daughters are worried about their safety on the ark because of the presence of the lion. Noah prayed to God for help, and God afflicted the lion with a fever. But not too much later another dangerous creature emerged: the mouse. Again Noah prayed, and this time, God caused the lion to sneeze and the cat issued forth.

In a medieval legend, the Devil plays a role in the creation of the cat. Trying to copy God and create a man, the evil Devil manages only to produce a small, pathetic, skinless animal, the cat. St. Peter felt sorry for the creature, and so he gave it a fur coat, which is the cat's only valuable possession. (From *The Quintessential Cat*, by Roberta Altman. New York: Macmillan, 1994.)

tethered to chairs in homes are found in Theban tombs dating from about 1450 B.C.

More than likely, the cat domesticated himself because the

arrangement was mutually beneficial. When humans turned from hunting game to cultivating crops, the harvest was a magnet to voracious vermin. The scurrying rodents that pilfered grain stores in turn drew wild cats to the feast. Humans soon learned that cats helped protect crops and food stores from the rodents, and so they encouraged the cats to stay.

The direct ancestry of the domestic house cat has long been argued. Today, most experts agree that the grand-daddy of all house cats is the African Wildcat. Slightly bigger than modern house cats, this big yellow tabby roams the deserts of Africa, Syria, Egypt and parts of India, and it matches the mummified remains of the domesticated cats of ancient Egypt.

Cat eyes have forever been symbols of grace, beauty and mysticism.

THE GLORY DAYS

Some civilizations invented glorious superhuman beings that combined human and feline characteristics, like the famous lion-man figure of the Sphinx at Giza, found outside Cairo, Egypt.

Affection for cats reached its zenith when Kitty was literally put on a pedestal. About 950 B.C., a city of the Nile delta called Bubastis worshipped a cat-headed goddess called Bast, or Pasht. She was the favorite of the sun god, Ra, and was associated with happiness, pleasure, dancing and the warmth of the sun.

GRACE AND BEAUTY

Feline grace was considered the epitome of beauty. The eyes of the African Wildcat are rimmed with a dark lining, and fine Egyptian ladies used cosmetics to outline their own eyes not only as protection from the sun, but perhaps to mimic the look of these cats. Egyptian law protected cats, and each one's death was greatly mourned. Cats were a jealously guarded treasure, and were not allowed to leave the country. But some were stolen and smuggled out by covetous visitors. Kitty traveled from

Egypt and was soon introduced around the world.

OUT OF EGYPT

Cats first traveled from Egypt to India, and from there to China and Japan. Although writings by Confucius indicate that he kept a pet cat in 500 B.C., cats were also treated as a delicacy in China and eaten. But in Japan, cats were held in such high esteem that they guarded precious manuscripts in pagodas, and for several centuries ownership was restricted to members of the Japanese nobility.

It was considered good luck if a cat crossed your path, and it was believed that light-colored cats brought their owners silver, while dark-colored cats brought them gold. So instrumental were cats in catching mice in silk factories that they're credited with saving the silk industry.

The next stop was Greece and Rome where cats were kept, along with ferrets, to guard the grain. Some people, though, seemed to appreciate Kitty for more than his mousing abilities. Scientists studying the entombed city of Pompeii found a woman who died in the lava while holding her pet cat in her arms.

A CAT BY ANY OTHER NAME

In English it's cat; in French, *chat*. The Germans call them *Katzen,* the Spanish and Syrians, *gatos,* and the Arabs, *qitt.* The ancient Byzantine word was *katos,* and the Latin *catus.* All are from *kadiz,* which was the word for cat in Nubia, an ancient Nile Valley kingdom that included southern Egypt.

The Greek fable writer Aesop included cats in a number of his works from the sixth century, B.C. Remember *The Cat and the Fox,* in which the cat "outsmarts" the sly fox himself? Or, *The Cat and the Mice,* in which an old cat tries to deceive her prey, but they don't take the bait? These stories were rooted in traits we associate with cats to this day: cleverness, quick thinking and secretiveness.

Cats were introduced into Northern Europe by the 10th century, probably by hitching rides on seafaring vessels. Crusaders who had traveled to the Middle East inadvertently brought back rats and house mice with them, and cats helped control these pests on the ships. In early England, cats were quite rare and were highly prized as rat catchers.

Myths and Superstitions About Cats

- A cat has nine lives.
- Cats' eyes shine at night because they are casting out the light they gathered during the day.
- When a cat's whiskers droop, rain is coming.
- If you want to keep a cat from straying, put butter on its feet.
- If a cat sneezes near a bride on her wedding day, she will have a happy marriage.
- A man who mistreats his cat will die in a storm.
- Stepping over a cat brings bad luck.

In America, Kitty earned his keep by policing haylofts and barnyards.

Laws of the day specified sizable fines for anyone who killed a cat.

To America

How did the domestic cat reach American shores? It had a transatlantic job to do: keep ships free of mice. And probably to keep the ship's passengers company as well. Though the northern native Americans did not seem to have domestic cats, some archaeologists believe that the cat was worshipped in Peru, South America. When early settlers' colonies became rat infested, the cat was called on again and gained a permanent place in North American homes.

Down on the Farm

Through the years, cats continued to be prized as guardians of grain and for running pest patrol in city warehouses.

A 1947 innovation, kitty litter, changed the lifestyle of cats forever. Before, Kitty performed potty duty outside, and the rare indoor cat settled for a box of sand or ashes. The convenience of new litter products moved many cats from the barnyard

Cats became major symbols of power and virility in ancient Egypt, and were much admired for their mystical qualities.

into the parlor. When dry and semi-moist cat foods appeared in the 1960s, cats were no longer kept strictly as mousers. Cats had become the pets of choice for the enlightened.

Despite a growing affection for them, little was known about cats. Cats, it was said, were independent little creatures who took care of themselves. Just 30 years ago, veterinarians were still treating cats the same as small dogs.

But soon their growing popularity made industry sit up and take notice. New products not only catered to existing feline fans; they encouraged others to discover the wonderful world of cats. During the 1970s,

By adopting your furry wonder, you've entered the enchanted world of cats.

scratching posts and creative litter pans designed to help outdoor cats transfer to an indoor lifestyle brought

BLACK CATS

Throughout time, black cats have been both praised as being bearers of great luck and persecuted as harbingers of grave misfortune. The word *felis* is Roman for a good and auspicious omen, though the Romans also called cats *gatta*, meaning weasel.

In the Middle Ages, black cats were associated with sorcery, and many were killed in symbolic ceremonies.

Black cats are linked to fate in many countries. In America, it's said that if a black cat crosses your path, it's bad luck; in Ireland, it foretells death in an epidemic; yet, in England and Asia, it means you will have great luck.

Black cats were kept by sailors' wives to ensure their husbands' safety, and they have starred in stories and poems by Edgar Allan Poe and William Butler Yeats.

owners closer to their cats, enriching the lives of both.

The decade also brought a wealth of feline medical advances, and cats became a veterinary specialty when the American Association of Feline Practitioners was founded in the early 1970s. These advances made sharing our lives with cats even more rewarding.

THE CITY KITTY

The 1980s brought increasing changes in social structures and lifestyles when people began, more and more, to live in cities and apartments. Cats were perceived to be convenience pets because they were just the right size for apartment living and didn't demand daily walks like dogs. Consequently, the late 1980s saw cats surpass dogs as the number one pet of choice in the United States.

About the same time, researchers began studying the human–companion animal bond and discovered what cat lovers had known all along: Cats are good for you. Stroking a cat lowers blood pressure. A cat in the house buffers stress, which reduces stress-related illness and can even prolong life. Kitty took the news in stride and began making day-trips to hospital wards as therapy animals. By 1994, the number of pet cats in the United States rose to 59.4 million.

Having crossed the threshold from barnyard to parlor, the cat has taken his rightful place as pampered pet. But more than that, your kitten will become a cherished friend—and a true member of the family.

CHAPTER EIGHT

On Good Behavior

"Train a cat?" you say. "Surely, you jest!" Actually, cats are extremely intelligent and learn very easily when something interests them. For instance, kittens quickly learn where their food is stored and how to open the cupboard door.

But unlike dogs, whose pack mentality prompts them to please humans, cats rarely relish obedience to another. In fact, cats train humans to believe they're untrainable so that owners don't expect good behavior from them. If your kitten is to be a welcome member of your family, though, she must learn a few simple rules.

RULES TO REMEMBER

First, correcting bad behavior after the fact will only confuse your kitten. She won't understand she's

With cats' non-chalant and inde-pendent attitudes, it is no wonder why many people are convinced that cats are untrainable.

being punished for shredding the newspaper if it happened hours ago. Corrections are effective only when you catch Kitty in the act.

Second, cats do not respond well to physical correction. Slapping or hitting simply makes Kitty fear your hands, something she'll remember the next time you want to pet her. It can also make aggressive cats strike back and become more aggressive, while irreparably traumatizing shy kittens.

The "No" Message

Verbal chastisement sometimes works, particularly with kittens. If

you're fortunate, a kitten's obedience to Momma-cat may be transferred to you. But don't shout at your cat; instead use an authoritative "No!" in response to poor behavior. Many kittens understand your meaning if you hiss at them, "SSSSSSST!" like Momma-cat did to signal inappro-priate behavior.

Don't chuckle or smile when you chastise, or Kitty will know you're more amused than aggravated. Be consistent: Don't let her do something one day, then scold her for it the next; changing the rules is confusing. Don't dwell on negatives, or she will learn that breaking rules is the best way to get attention, even if the attention is negative.

The "Yes" Message

Reward good behavior with effusive praise. Talk to your kitten and tell her what a smart, wonderful cat she is and why. Most cats learn to understand many human words, and the more they know, the fewer misunderstandings and opportunities for misbehavior there will be.

The easiest way to train a cat is to make the desired behavior more fun than the alternative. Cats respond best to positive reinforcement like treats, playtime and owner attention.

Finally, when correction is necessary, don't let Kitty know it came from you. To your cat, you are the source of comfort, love, good food and fun times. Negative reinforcement should seem to arise from the "unknown," the Almighty Invisible Paw of the Cat-God. Otherwise, Kitty will behave only when you're in the vicinity and ignore the rules when you're out of range.

Booby traps, long-distance squirt guns, loud noises and other harmless unpleasantness persuade Kitty it's really not so much fun after all to leap on the counter, swing from the tablecloth or scratch the sofa.

USING THE LITTER BOX

By about three weeks of age, kittens begin imitating Momma. They taste and mouth her food, lick themselves and each other, and follow her to

Giving treats to your kitten is an effective way to reinforce good behavior.

the litter box. With few exceptions, kittens will already know what litter is for by following Momma-cat's example.

Some kittens will need a little help in the potty department, though. Just as with opening a business, the three most important issues in litter box training are location, location, location. Even if the kitten understands what to do with litter, you must make sure she knows where the box is and that she can get to it in time. The litter box should be convenient for her to use but some distance away from eating and sleeping areas, or you'll offend her sense of kitty decorum. A low-traffic area that provides some privacy is perfect.

Keep about 2 inches of clean litter in the box. Cats like monotony, so once you've found an acceptable litter, don't switch brands unless you must. Sudden change may upset your kitten and disrupt bathroom habits, and then neither of you will be happy.

Encourage Good Habits

Right after a meal, a potty break is often imminent. After the first few meals, either set your kitten on the litter or let her climb in by herself. Encourage Kitty to scratch and sniff about by digging in the litter with your finger. She should quickly get the right idea. Wait until she finishes, then offer lots of verbal praise.

From a very early age, your kitten will know that the proper place to eliminate is in her litter box.

It's important that the litter box remain clean, but for the first week or so, leave your kitten's freshest deposit behind as a fragrant reminder. Let her follow you away from the box so that she'll learn its location. Soon, she'll follow you to the box after each meal or head off for a private session on her own when she feels the need.

CLAWING CONDUCT

Clawing is normal feline behavior, and you cannot—nor should you—train the behavior away. The trick is to redirect Kitty's needle-sharp claws away from your furniture and give her another, better scratching outlet.

Place the scratching post in a convenient area near Kitty's bed or food bowl (cats enjoy a good scratch after eating or sleeping). If it's stuck away in the corner of an empty room, don't expect her to hunt it down; she'd rather stay with you and use your footstool.

Make It a Game

To begin, make scratching a game. Direct your kitten's attention to the post, using a peacock feather or another irresistible kitten toy. Tease her with the fluttering feather all around the scratching post, playing hide and seek. Your kitten will naturally grab the post as she tries to catch the feather. Demonstrate what you want and scratch it yourself; then praise when she scratches.

Whenever you catch your kitten flexing claws somewhere she shouldn't, hiss or tell her "No!" and gently move her to the post. Your kitten may get the idea faster if a vertical post is set on its side so that she can actually sit on the post and dig in.

Enforcing the Message

Always praise your kitten when she chooses the correct scratching apparatus. With some consistency, Kitty will learn what prompts praise.

Treating the post with catnip will attract most adult cats but not kittens. Catnip is an acquired taste that comes with maturity, and even then, not all cats react to it.

LET THEM LEAD

Cats tend to tolerate and even relish leash walks when they lead the way.

83

They stroll and will not be rushed, indulging in a sniff here and a pause there, investigating a dragonfly or the rustle of mousy interlopers. Trying to force a faster pace generally results in Kitty putting on the brakes. Cats quite literally stop to smell the roses . . . and the sidewalk, your shoe, the leaves . . .

Start Young

Leash training gives your cat the pleasure of safely supervised outdoor excursions. For health reasons, however, you should wait to go outside until your kitten has had all her shots.

Leash training isn't for all cats, nor is the outdoors. Some cats are

Much patience is necessary to acclimate a cat to the whole idea of a harness and lead.

perfectly content to keep carpet beneath their paws their whole life long and are terrified without a roof between them and the sky.

An invaluable tool used by trainers of animal actors is a simple handheld clicker. The clicker is used in combination with bits of canned cat food (tiny pieces!) that Kitty particularly likes. The sound reinforces and signals that she's done something right. She does not have to be hungry to respond, so don't think you have to deny her dinner.

Train Slowly

All initial training takes place in the safety of your house. First, leave the leash and harness out for Kitty to investigate on her own. After she's thoroughly sniffed it, rubbed it and decided it's no threat, you're ready for the next step: donning the equipment.

This is a big deal for kittens. Have your treats ready, then put the harness on your kitten. Don't bother yet with the leash. If you're fortunate, she will consider the halter a wonderful new game, and it won't slow her down. But many kittens roll and meow in distress, trying to scrape the harness off.

It won't be long before your kitten is walking, sniffing, listening and watching on your walks.

Regardless of how Kitty reacts to wearing the harness, tempt her to walk by waving the treat under her nose. When she stands and walks with the harness on, praise her, click the clicker, and give her the treat. You should give the click and treat simultaneously, but only as a reward for performing correctly. Give Kitty the click-treat each time she stands up and walks to you, but do not give a click-treat unless she stands up and walks.

Adding the Leash

Leave the harness on for 10 minutes, two to three times a day. Again, reward with a click-treat only when Kitty walks while wearing it. When she appears comfortable with the harness, simply attach the leash and let her drag it about the room. She may revert to rolling, or it may not faze her at all. As before, reward her when she's vertical and moving.

Then pick up the end of the leash. Loop the end securely about one hand, and control the slack with the other. Give her roaming room, but offer a gentle tug now and again to guide her. When she responds to the tug and follows your direction, give her a click-treat reward. Repeat the exercise for short periods two to three times a day until Kitty is comfortable.

Out You Go!

Finally, if your kitten is old enough (at least 16 weeks old) and has had all protective shots, you're ready for the outdoors. Walk the route first by yourself so that you can avoid barking dogs, heavy traffic or other hazards. Choose a quiet park or your backyard for your strolls. Slowly phase out click-treat rewards.

COMING WHEN CALLED

Yes, cats can be trained to come when called. This can be particularly helpful when you need to find your cat quickly. And if you've had your kitten any length of time, you know there's one sure-fire thing that brings her running. Food.

A well-trained kitten is a pleasure to live with.

Were cats not safely confined to their individual houses, the sound of the can opener would bring them running from miles away. Use that simple principle, coupled with click-treat rewards, to bring your kitten running at other times as well.

As you prepare her meal and she's running to you, call her name, saying, "Kitty, come!" When she arrives, give her a click-treat and set down the food. Do this every time she's fed, and soon she'll relate her name being called with a food reward. The clicker lets her know she's done what you wanted.

Then try calling her at times other than mealtimes. When she comes running, have the click-treat ready. Make it a game, crossing to the other side of the room or hiding behind a chair, calling, "Kitty, come!" and having her come to different locations to receive a click-treat.

Once she's coming consistently, you'll want to phase out the click-treats and reward her only occasionally. Intermittent reinforcement is a much more powerful training tool: Because she never knows when she'll get rewarded, she tries every time.

CHAPTER NINE

Resources

BOOKS

About Felines

Church, Christine. *Housecat.* New York: Howell Book House, 1998.

Commings, Karen. *Shelter Cats.* New York: Howell Book House, 1998.

Edney, Andrew. *ASPCA Complete Cat Care Manual.* New York: Houghton Mifflin, 1993.

Fox, Dr. Michael. *Supercat: Raising the Perfect Feline Companion.* New York: Howell Book House, 1990.

Gebhart, Richard. *The Complete Cat Book.* New York: Howell Book House, 1995.

Hammond, Sean, and Carolyn Usrey. *How to Raise a Sane and Healthy Cat.* New York: Howell Book House, 1994.

Janike, Carolyn and Ruth Rgnis. *The Complete Idiot's Guide to Living with a Cat.* New York: Howell Book House, 1998.

Jankowski, Connie. *Adopting Cats and Kittens.* New York: Howell Book House, 1993.

Mallone, John. *The 125 Most Asked Questions About Cats (and the Answers).* New York: William Morrow and Company, Inc., 1992.

Shojai, Amy. *The Cat Companion: The History, Culture, and Everyday Life of the Cat.* New York: Mallard Press, 1992.

About Health Care

Carlson, Delbert, DVM, and James Giffin, MD. *Cat Owner's Home Veterinary Handbook.* New York: Howell Book House, 1995.

Evans, J. M., and Kay White. *Catlopaedia.* New York: Howell Book House, 1997.

Evans, Mark. *The Complete Guide to Kitten Care.* New York: Howell Book House, 1996.

Hawcroft, Tim, BVSc. (Hons), MACVs. *First Aid for Cats: The Essential Quick-Reference Guide.* New York: Howell Book House, 1994.

McGinnis, Terri. *Well Cat Book.* New York: Random House, 1993.

Wexler-Mitchell, Elaine. *The Complete Idiot's Guide to a Healthy Cat.* New York: Howell Book House, 1999.

About Training

Eckstein, Warren and Fay. *How to Get Your Cat to Do What You Want.* New York: Villard Books, 1990.

Fogle, Bruce, DVM, MRCVs. *The Cat's Mind: Understanding Your Cat's Behavior.* New York: Howell Book House, 1992.

Franklin, Sally. *50 Ways to Train Your Cat.* New York: Howell Book House, 1996.

Johnson, Pam (Feline Behavior Consultant*). Twisted Whiskers: Solving Your Cat's Behavior Problems.* Freedom, CA: The Crossing Press, 1994.

Smith, Carin A. *101 Training Tips for Your Cat.* New York: DTP, 1994.

Whiteley, E. H. *Understanding and Training Your Cat or Kitten.* New York: Crown Publishing Group, 1994.

Wright, John C., M.A., Ph.D., and Judy Wright Lashnits. *Is Your Cat Crazy? Behavior Problems and Solutions from the Casebook of a Cat Therapist.* New York: Macmillan, 1994.

MAGAZINES

Cat Fancy. P.O. Box 6050, Mission Viejo, CA 92690 (714-855-8822).

Catnip (Newsletter of Tufts University Medical Center). P.O. Box 420014, Palm Coast, FL 32142-0014 (800-829-0926).

CATS. P.O. Box 290037, Port Orange, FL 32129 (904-788-2770).

Cat World International. P.O. Box 35635, Phoenix, AZ 85069 (602-995-1822)

Just Cats. Box 1831, New Fairfield, CT 06812 (203-746-6760).

Meow (Newsletter of the Cat Writer's Association), P.O. Box 351, Trilby, FL 33593-0351 (904-583-3744).

Pawprints. P.O. Box 833, North Hollywood, CA 91603 (818-360-4068).

89

MORE INFORMATION ABOUT FELINES

Clubs

American Cat Fanciers Association
P.O. Box 203
Point Lookout, MO 65726
(417) 334-5430
(417) 334-5540 (fax)
www.acfacat.com

Cat Fanciers' Association, Inc.
P.O. Box 1005
Manasquan, NJ 08736-0805
(732) 528-9797
(732) 528-7391 (fax)
www.cfainc.org/cfa/

American Cat Association
8101 Katherine Ave.
Panorama City, CA 91402
(818) 782-6080

Canadian Cat Association
220 Advance Blvd., Suite 101
Brampton, Ontario
Canada L6T 4J5
(905) 459-1481
(905) 459-4023 (fax)
www.cca-afc.com

Other Associations

The Winn Feline Foundation for the Health and Well-Being of Cats
1805 Atlantic Ave.
P.O. Box 1005
Manasquan, NJ 08736
(908) 528-9797

Cat Writers Association
Cheryl Smith, Secretary
496 Gasman Rd.
Port Angeles, WA 98362

OTHER USEFUL RESOURCES— WEB SITES

General

www.cathalloffame.com
The Cat Hall of Fame
Fun site dedicated to all things feline.

www.fanciers.com
Web site of the Cat Fanciers Mailing List, a group committed to bettering the lives of all cats. Includes numerous links to other Web sites and information about breeding, showing, health and rescue.

www.catwriters.org
Cat Writers' Association
The Cat Writers' Association is a professional organization of cat communication: writers, editors, publishers, artists, public relation specialists and broadcasters.

Health and Breed Rescue

http://web.vet.cornell.edu/public/fhc/ FelineHealth.html
Cornell University Feline Health Ctr.

http://netvet.wustl.edu
NetVet Veterinary Resources

www.ecn.purdue.edu/~laird/ animal_rescue
Animal Rescue Resources

Other Links

Here are some links to other interesting Web sites:

www.best.com/~sirlou
acemepet.com
iviallage.pet
pets.com
about.com